PELICAN BOOKS
A208
THE ENGLISH PARLIAMENT
K. R. MACKENZIE

In honour of

THOMAS MORE

Speaker, Chancellor, Saint

THE
ENGLISH PARLIAMENT

K. R. MACKENZIE

PENGUIN BOOKS
BALTIMORE · MARYLAND

Penguin Books Ltd, Harmondsworth, Middlesex
U.S.A.: Penguin Books Inc., 3300 Clipper Mill Road, Baltimore 11, Md
AUSTRALIA: Penguin Books Pty Ltd, 762 Whitehorse Road,
Mitcham, Victoria

—

First published 1950
Revised and reprinted 1951, 1959, 1962, 1963

—

Copyright © K. R. Mackenzie, 1950

—

Made and printed in Great Britain
by The Whitefriars Press Ltd, London and Tonbridge
Set in Monotype Baskerville
Collogravure plates by Harrison & Sons Ltd

*I doubt that the most important thing was Dunkirk or the Battle
of Britain, El Alamein or Stalingrad. Not even the landings in
Normandy or the great blows struck by British and American
bombers. Historians may decide that any one of these events was
decisive, but I am persuaded that the most important thing that
happened in Britain was that this nation chose to win or lose this
war under the established rules of parliamentary procedure. It
feared Nazism, but did not choose to imitate it. The government
was given dictatorial power, but it was used with restraint, and
the House of Commons was ever vigilant. Do you remember that
while London was being bombed in the daylight, the House
devoted two days to discussing conditions under which enemy
aliens were detained on the Isle of Man? Though Britain fell,
there were to be no concentration camps here.*

EDWARD R. MURROW
Broadcast, February 1946

Contents

LIST OF ILLUSTRATIONS BETWEEN
PAGES 104 AND 105

1. The Opening of Parliament in 1523
2. The House of Commons in 1640
3. The House of Commons in 1741/2
4. The House of Lords in 1755. The King sitting on the Throne, the Commons attending him at the end of the Session
5. The House of Lords in 1808
6. The House of Commons in 1808
7. The Reformed House of Commons, 1834
8. The House of Commons, May 7th, 1940 (After the painting by John Worsley)

Preface

The purpose of this book is not to describe How We are Governed or the Way Parliament Works. It is rather an attempt to explain how parliament came to be what it is – the origins of its character in English history. For it is England which is the mother of parliaments.

The arrangement is not strictly chronological, nor yet simply by subjects. Each period has made its special contribution to the development of the institution; each chapter, except the eighth (The Independence of the Speaker) and the twelfth (The Second Chamber), concentrates on the special contribution of one such period.

I am greatly indebted and wish to record my sincere thanks to Mr E. A. Fellowes, the Clerk Assistant of the House of Commons, for overlooking the work from its earliest stages; to Professor Sir Frank Stenton for explaining the relation of the Norman Great Council to the *witenagemot*; to Sir Cecil Carr for scrutinizing the chapter on delegated legislation; to Mr L. A. Abraham for pointing out some of the gaps in my knowledge; and to Mr E. Ballard, Mr K. A. Bradshaw, Mr B. St G. Drennan, and Mr J. P. S. Taylor for their kind help in various ways. It goes without saying that none of these gentlemen accepts any responsibility for the defects which remain.

I have to thank the Lord Great Chamberlain and the Serjeant at Arms for permission to photograph those pictures which hang in the Palace of Westminster, and the Trustees of the British Museum for permission to reproduce the engraving of the House of Commons in 1640.

For the picture of the House of Commons on May 7th, 1940, I am much indebted to the kindness of Mr John

Worsley, the artist; to Time-Life International Limited for
their courtesy in allowing me to reproduce it; and to Studio
Sun Limited for lending me a photograph of it.

I am most grateful to Mr Edward Murrow for permission
to quote the closing sentences from his farewell broadcast
and to the British Broadcasting Corporation who first gave
them to the world.

I should also like to express my appreciation of the helpful-
ness and forbearance of the staff of Penguin Books Limited
in the production of this book.

My indebtedness to the writings of modern historians is
indicated by the lists of authorities at the ends of chapters
II, V, VIII, X, XI, and XII. In particular I have to acknowledge my debt to Mr C. S. Emden and the Clarendon
Press for the use in chapters VI and VII of material derived
from *The People and the Constitution*.

K. R. M.

WESTMINSTER,
  9 *July* 1949.

CHAPTER I

A COURT BECOMES
A PARLIAMENT

The one thing that saved England from the fate of other countries
was not her insular position, nor the independent spirit nor the magnanimity of her people – for we have been proud of the despotism we
obeyed under the Tudors, and not ashamed of the tyranny we exercised
in our dependencies – but only the consistent, uninventive, stupid
fidelity to that political system which originally belonged to all the
nations that traversed the ordeal of feudalism.   LORD ACTON

Moreover, the King has over him a court, that is to say the earls and
barons; for the earls, as their name (*comites*) implies, are the com-
panions of the King, and he who has a colleague has a master.

BRACTON

PARLIAMENT IS FEUDAL

IT is no antiquarian pedantry that traces the origin of
parliament back to Saxon times. For the tradition that the
king must govern with the advice of his great men was
already well established when the Conqueror arrived, and
his Great Council not only included men who had been of
the Council of Edward the Confessor, but was rightly
regarded by Englishmen as the constitutional equivalent of
the *witena gemot*.

Feudalism was basically a system of land tenure by which
the freeman held land from his lord in return for certain
services – military and other – and the lord in his turn owed
service to the king as overlord. But it was much more than
a system of land tenure. Feudalism was a whole way of life –
a social system in which lord and vassal were bound together
by the closest possible ties. In the oath of homage the vassal
swore 'to become your man for the tenement I hold of you

and to bear faith to you of life and members and earthly
honour against all other men.' The lord on his part undertook to maintain his vassal in his tenement and to defend
him in law against all other men. The effect of this relationship was to bring into being a community of tenants with
the lord at its centre. This community, the honour as it
was called, found its concrete expression in the honorial
court, to which the tenants were bound to come and
wherein the lord was entitled to their advice. When
therefore, as we are told, the Conqueror asserted his lordship over every acre of the land, he thereby brought into
being a single feudal community, the honour of England.
His vassals, *alias* tenants-in-chief, *alias* barons, as members
of this feudal community, owed duty of attendance and
advice in the royal court. This is what Thomas Becket
meant when he wrote to King Henry 'In that you are
my lord, I owe and offer you counsel.' He may have been
somewhat ironical, but he was in fact only stating plainly
the duty of a feudal vassal in a feudal court – to advise.

Royal courts were held thrice a year on the solemn
occasions at Christmas, Easter and Whitsun when the Norman kings wore their crowns. The chronicler tells us that
there were present 'all the great men of England, archbishops, bishops, abbots, earls, thegns and knights.' We
know that from the earliest times a special writ of summons[1]
was sent to each tenant-in-chief and there were penalties for
non-attendance. At these courts pleas were judged and decisions taken on matters of state. The tradition of these great
courts at the crown-wearings was never quite lost. A
hundred years later, in 1176, Henry II held his Christmas
court at Nottingham and immediately afterwards held a
great council with bishops, earls and barons of the kingdom,
at which various great business was done; and when, in the
middle of the next century (in 1258), the barons at Oxford

1. The earliest extant is of 1204–5.

demanded three parliaments a year they were harking back to the old thrice-yearly crown-wearing courts.

In the intervals between these great national assemblies, and for the ordinary business of government, the king relied upon a small number of personal advisers. These advisers, variously called *familiares*, *domestici*, *ministri*, were, as the terms imply, members of the royal household and essentially, therefore, royal servants. In the Norman and Angevin periods these household officers were normally drawn from the ranks of the baronage, but with the growing complexity of administration, several of the most important offices, notably those of the chancellor, the treasurer and the justices, came to be held by officials – men of non-baronial rank with professional qualifications. At the same time, in the reign of John or during the minority of Henry III, this little group of personal advisers [1] began to acquire an organization of its own and we can speak of a 'council' rather than of 'counsellors'.

Thus at the very outset of our inquiry we are confronted by a distinction which is vital for the understanding of parliamentary history. On the one hand a general assembly of the tenants-in-chief, wherein the whole nation was conceived to be present, meets at intervals to advise the king on the greatest matters. On the other hand, a small body of personal advisers assists the king in the actual day-to-day business of government. Parliament is the child of the occasional national assembly and retains to-day its essential character as an advisory – critical if you like – assembly representative of the nation. In the course of time it has found the means to enforce its advice and to make its criticism effective, but it does not itself govern. The king and his private council have developed into the whole complex

1. 'The persons assisting us by whose advice the affairs of our kingdom are disposed', as Henry III referred to them in a letter. *Royal Letters*, II, p. 303.

machine which we call 'the government', i.e. the ministry and the civil service. This distinction – between legislature and executive in modern parlance – is basic to the whole conception of parliamentary government. Though the elements were present in this early period, it was many centuries before they were clearly recognized. In fact, the history of parliament might be described in terms of the strains and stresses involved in the adjustment of their proper relation to each other.

What is a parliament? What was it that converted the feudal great council into 'parliament'? Certainly not the summoning of the Commons, since the word came into use to describe assemblies consisting only of the king, his personal advisers, and the prelates, earls and barons – fifty years before the summoning of the Commons became the usual practice.

The earliest document in which the word 'parliament' is found is the eleventh-century *Chanson de Roland*, where it is used simply of a conversation between two persons. 'I cannot hold long *parlement* with you', says the emir Baligant to the dying king Marsile. But the word early acquired a derivative meaning, that of an assembly of persons in which discussion takes place. In the twelfth century general assemblies in the Italian cities were called *parlamenti*, and writers of this period used the word to describe such meetings as those in which Harold took his oath to William and Henry disputed with Becket at Northampton. A contemporary referred to the meeting of barons at Runnymede, at which King John gave the Great Charter, as a 'parliament'. Clearly the essence of parliament is discussion, and when the word is first applied to the great councils of the English Kings it is in order to emphasize their deliberative function.

In 1232 Henry III, declaring himself of age, forthwith dis-

missed the counsellors who had conducted the government
during the regency and installed in their place foreigners of
his own choosing. In so doing he did nothing that he was
not entitled to do – the choice of his immediate advisers was
his own personal affair. The fact that they were foreigners,
however distasteful, gave the English barons no ground for
complaint on feudal or, as we should say, constitutional
principles. It was only when Henry proceeded to conduct
the government entirely without consulting them as his
'natural counsellors' on the most important matters that the
barons had a real grievance. Such matters in their opinion
were the marriage of Henry's sister to the Emperor and the
negotiation of the alliance with Poitou, both of which had
been undertaken without their approval. Their indignation
was not allayed when they came to Westminster and found
that Henry had removed to the Tower, whence he would
only communicate with them through one of his clerks. The
climax of outrage was reached in 1237, when Henry summoned the barons to a great council, at which they were only
asked to grant an aid and no great business was put before
them. 'Are we not among the number of the king's friends?'
it was asked. What we want, they seem to have said, is a full
discussion of the affairs of the realm – in fact a *colloquium*, and
this is the word which Matthew Paris, the contemporary
chronicler, begins to use in this year to describe the assemblies of the barons. Five years later *parliamentum*, a more
popular and less formal equivalent of *colloquium*, appears
in an official document to describe a great council to which
the king summoned prelates, earls and barons to discuss
'our difficult business, touching the state of us and our
whole kingdom'. By 1258 parliament has evidently begun
to acquire a special meaning. The assembly which met at
Easter, 1258, is perhaps the first we are justified in regarding
as certainly a true parliament, and in June of the same
year one of the reforms demanded by the barons at Oxford

was for three parliaments a year 'to treat of the business of the king and the kingdom'.

From 1258 onwards it is possible to establish with more or less certainty the list of true parliaments. For parliaments were summoned by a special kind of writ which distinguished them from other kinds of national assembly. A parliamentary writ invited the recipient to discuss not merely with the king but with the other magnates, and the business to be discussed was not merely the king's business but the business of the king and the kingdom. In other words, the appearance of the word 'parliament' indicated a recognition of the right of feudal counsellors not merely to tender individual advice to the king but to discuss with each other. Inevitably, the effect was to crystallize that duality which, we have suggested, is the essence of parliamentary government. The magnates were still only advisers summoned at the royal discretion, but the invitation to discuss with each other evidently conceded to them a degree of corporate existence which could not fail in the long run to encourage their development as the critics of, rather than the participators in, government.

THE ARRIVAL OF THE COMMONS

THE same quarrel which precipitated the baronial demand for parliament led not so many years later to the summoning of the Commons. In 1254 the king, being in Gascony, demanded through his regents an aid on the ground that he was about to be attacked by the King of Castile. The prelates were willing to grant an aid, but would give no undertaking on behalf of the clergy without their consent. The earls and barons also promised an aid, but it was reported to the king that he would not be able to get an aid from the rest of the laity, unless he gave emphatic orders to his lieutenants in England strictly to observe the great charter of liberties and unless he proclaimed the same in all the counties in England. In these circumstances the bishops were ordered to assemble their diocesan synods and to persuade them to grant an aid which should be stated before the council by trustworthy persons; and the sheriffs were likewise ordered to send to the council two legal and discreet knights elected by each county on behalf of all and each (*vice omnium et singulorum*) 'to consider together with the knights of the other counties whom we have had summoned for the same day, what aid they will be willing to grant us in our great need'. The sheriff was also bidden to explain the king's difficulties and his urgent need to the knights and other inhabitants of the county, 'so that the said knights shall be able on the date fixed to answer exactly to our council in the name of the counties'.

The meeting to which knights of the shire were summoned was almost certainly not a parliament, since its purpose was merely that they might report to the king and council the amount of a subsidy which had already been agreed upon at an earlier council of magnates. But the circumstances are illuminating. They show that the reason for summoning the representatives of the shires was financial, and a precedent was set for similar summonses in the future. Seven years later, when Henry and the barons were at open war, both sides sought the support of the shires and issued competing writs to the sheriffs directing them to send knights to a national assembly. In 1264, after his victory at Lewes, Simon de Montfort issued writs in the king's name, ordering the election of four lawful and discreet knights by each shire to discuss the state of the realm; and in 1265 he summoned to his second parliament not only two knights from each county but also two citizens from each city and two burgesses from each borough. The Commons had arrived. Who were the Commons?

The Shires. Older than Alfred, to whom their institution was popularly ascribed, the shires had been the unit area of Anglo-Saxon local government, and the shire court, in which knights and freemen attended, was the organ of local justice and administration. The Norman settlement arrested their development as centres of local authority, but when Henry II sent his justices into the shire courts, their corporate identity began to revive. Legal community led naturally to political community. The shires began to petition for local liberties, to claim an increasing share of local government and to secure the choice of their own officers. The shires in fact became fully developed communities – *communes* – 'Commons'.

At the same time the shires began to acquire fiscal unity. In the eleventh century the tenant-in-chief was the normal intermediary for the collection of feudal dues from the knights and free tenants, while the sheriffs collected revenues due to the king from his own domain lands. King John, with characteristic contempt for feudal principle, broke away from this system. In 1207 he instituted what was in fact the first national tax, as opposed to a feudal due, by exacting a shilling in the mark,[1] loosely called a thirteenth, upon the chattels of every layman, within or without the royal domain lands. This tax (which in the thirteenth century became the principal source of revenue) was naturally based upon the shires, and its collection and assessment was entrusted to commissions of knights and freeholders. In 1213 John summoned four knights from each shire to Oxford 'to speak with us about the business of our kingdom'. It is not hard to guess what that formula meant. The business was financial. This was the precedent for the summons to the knights in 1254.

---

1. The mark was 13s. 4d.

The Boroughs. Like the shires, the boroughs were a pre-Conquest institution and had, in the course of the centuries, gradually achieved a measure of self-government, acquiring charters and the right to elect their own officers. Like the shires, too, but by a somewhat different process, they had acquired the right to assess their own taxes. They too were communities – *communes.* It was only natural that Simon de Montfort should call on them also for support.

Not without justification has Simon de Montfort been called the founder of the Commons. Nevertheless, the claim is a little too high, for after Simon's defeat at Evesham we have no evidence of their summons to any of the later parliaments of Henry III. De Montfort after all was a revolutionary and a rebel, and the parliament he called in 1265 was more like a party conference than a genuinely national assembly.

The Parliaments of Edward I. Edward I succeeded to the throne in 1272, and, on his return from Palestine three years later, held his 'first general parliament'. Knights, citizens and burgesses[1] were summoned 'to discuss together with the magnates the affairs of our kingdom'. A grant was made, but we may well believe that Edward's purpose in summoning the knights and burgesses was more than merely financial, and that their moral as well as their financial support was sought for the royal policies. It was the first time that the Commons were included in a genuinely national council.

Nevertheless it was by no means yet the rule to summon the Commons to every parliament. In the first twenty-five years of Edward I's reign some thirty parliaments were summoned, but there is evidence of the attendance of the Commons at only four.

1. 'Four knights more discreet in the law and also six or four citizens, burgesses or other honest men from each of the cities.'

The year 1295 was critical. The Welsh had rebelled, there was war with the Scots, and the French had landed at Dover. A parliament was necessary. The unusual wording of the writs of summons reflects the urgency of the situation. Beginning with an appeal to the ancient Roman maxim, 'That which touches all should be approved by all', the writs set forth the danger to the realm in great detail. The composition of the parliament was also unusual. Not only were knights, citizens and burgesses summoned, but also, for the first time, the representatives of the lower clergy. Subsidies were granted by the barons and knights together, by the clergy, and by the citizens and burgesses. The parliament of 1295 was in fact the most fully representative that had ever been called, and was evidently designed to mobilize the whole financial resources of the nation. But whether this parliament deserves to be called the 'Model' is perhaps doubtful, since less than forty years afterwards the representatives of the inferior clergy, whose presence was its chief claim to originality, ceased to attend parliaments.

The withdrawal of the lower clergy and the coalescence of knights with citizens and burgesses. The appearance of representatives of the lower clergy in parliament, though only a brief interlude in parliamentary history, is of interest for the light it throws on the motive for summoning the Commons, and also because their disappearance from parliament contributed towards the formation of the knights and burgesses into a single 'House'. Representatives of the lower clergy were first summoned to that national assembly of 1254, which, we have already suggested, was the precedent for Simon de Montfort's parliaments. They were present in the 'Model' parliament, as we have seen, and in other parliaments of the next twenty years. But from the beginning they showed a marked reluctance to participate in parliaments. No more than the knights and burgesses at this period were they inclined to regard attendance in parlia-

ment as a privilege: the summons was rather an augury
of burdens to be borne and attendance, to say the least, an
irksome duty. In 1315 the Chaplain of Christ Church,
Canterbury, when ordered by the Archbishop to send a
proctor, protested that parliament is 'a secular court, begun
and continued in the King's Chamber'. In 1321 the presence of the clergy was insisted on to ensure the validity of
the proceedings against the Despencers. But it is significant
that in 1322 the Statute of York did not include the lower
clergy among the estates whose consent is necessary in
matters touching the king and the realm. After 1332 the
proctors are not mentioned in the Rolls of Parliament.
From this time the clergy retained the right to tax themselves in convocation until 1664, when they submitted to
taxation at the same rate and in the same measure as the
laity. At the same time the lower clergy assumed, and they
have ever since enjoyed, the right of voting in the election
of members of the House of Commons.

The withdrawal of the inferior clergy helped to make possible the formation of the Commons into one body. When
knights, citizens and burgesses first came to parliament,
there is little evidence of corporate consciousness. At one
moment, indeed, it looked as if the social superiority of the
knights of the shires to the citizens and burgesses might result in the formation of a separate 'estate' or 'house'. In the
reign of Edward I the knights regularly made their grant at
the same rate as the barons, while the rest of the Commons
made a separate grant at a higher rate, and to the end of
Edward III's reign it remained a possibility that the knights
might make their grant at the lower rate. In 1372 the burgesses were actually detained in parliament to make a grant
after the dismissal of the knights. Nevertheless, from the accession of Edward III the evidence of co-operation between
the knights and the citizens and burgesses grows. The appearance at this time of *communes petitiones* suggests common

deliberation by the whole body of Commons. In 1332 and in 1339 the knights certainly acted with the *gentz de la Commune*, and thereafter knights, citizens and burgesses regularly deliberated together. The election from 1376 onwards of one of their number [1] to report their answers to the king in parliament marks a further stage in the process by which the Commons became a distinct entity. Yet in 1382 the Commons prayed, 'that the Prelates by themselves, the great temporal Lords by themselves, the Knights by themselves, the Justices by themselves, and all the other Estates separately, be charged to treat and consider of their charge', and separate action by knights on the one hand and citizens and burgesses on the other was possible as late as 1523.

The expression 'Estates of the Realm' came into use in the first half of the fifteenth century. After a certain hesitation as to its precise definition, it came usually to mean the Lords Spiritual, the Lords Temporal and the Commons. The expression 'House' appears in the latter half of the century. In 1450, 'the Speaker of the Parliament opened and declared (the charges against the Duke of Suffolk) in the Commons House' and 'there were sent unto the said Chancellor certain of the said House'. A 'House of Lords' is not heard of until the reign of Henry VIII.

The meeting place of the Commons. Our earliest information about the meeting place of the Commons, when they began to deliberate apart, comes from the Easter parliament of 1341. On the first day the cause of summons was announced by the Chancellor to the whole body of parliament, prelates and magnates, knights, citizens and burgesses, in the Painted Chamber.[2] The prelates and magnates were ordered

1. For the development of the Speakership see Chapter VIII below.

2. The Painted Chamber, the White Chamber and the Little Hall were in the oldest part of the Palace of Westminster, which lay to the south of Westminster Hall.

to assemble on a later day in the White Chamber to discuss
the matters proposed to them, and the knights of the counties and the Commons likewise to assemble in the Painted
Chamber. In 1352 the main body of the Commons was
ordered to betake itself to the Chapter House of the Abbey,
while 24 or 30 of their number discussed the king's business
with a delegation of the Lords in the Painted Chamber.[1]
In 1368 the Commons were assigned the Little Hall,
but in 1376 and 1377 the Chapter House is described as
'their former place'. The unprecedented length of the
Commons' session – ten weeks – in the Good Parliament
doubtless accounts for the reference in the Abbey Sacrist's
Roll for 1377–8 to the wearing out of certain floor-coverings
by a recent session of the Commons. The Commons used
the Chapter House again in 1384, but after 1395 this building disappears from the record. In the parliaments of the
next twenty years we find the Commons using the Refec-
tory of the Abbey. Where the Commons met during the
next 130 years is not recorded. In 1547, by the Second
Chantries Act, the chapel of St Stephen within the Palace
of Westminster fell to the king, who thereupon handed it
over to the Commons for their permanent use. There the
Commons sat for nearly 300 years until its destruction by
fire in 1834.[2]

1. These 'joint committees' of Lords and Commons are recorded in
twelve of the parliaments between 1352 and 1407. The Commons not
only chose the members of their own delegation but often actually named
the Lords whom they wished to meet; and on the two occasions when
the discussions are recorded, 1352 and 1376, the Commons clearly took
the lead. See *The Commons in Medieval English Parliaments*, by J. G.
Edwards, 1958.

2. See Plates 2, 3, 6 and 7.

CHAPTER II

THE COMMONS BECOME LEGISLATORS

The king has his court in his council, in his parliaments, in the presence of the prelates, earls, barons, lords and others learned in the law, where doubts about sentences are determined, where new remedies are provided for new injuries that have happened, and where justice is meted out to each according to his deserts.   FLETA

THE POSITION OF THE COMMONS

THE Commons had arrived in parliament – more truthfully, they were summoned to parliament whenever their presence was required, that is, whenever the king needed money. Throughout the reign of Edward I the Commons, whenever they are summoned, are only there 'to consent to whatever should be decided' on behalf of the shires and towns. Unlike the Lords, whose place in parliament was firmly based on their feudal claim to be the king's natural counsellors, the Commons owed such place in it as they had to the desirability, or the necessity it may be, of getting their agreement to financial exactions.

In the reign of Edward II, parliament continued to be a predominantly baronial institution, but the conception of parliament as representing the nation was growing, and the presence of the Commons therein was becoming increasingly usual. In his coronation oath Edward swore not only to keep the laws and customs granted by his predecessors, but also 'the laws and customs which the community of the realm shall have chosen'. The latter promise was new and seems to indicate a new attitude to the will of the community. But the expression 'the community of the realm' was an old one. In the past an assembly consisting only of magnates had been regarded as sufficiently representative of the community. Nor on the present occasion is there any reason to suppose that any wider conception was intended. Nevertheless, the phrase contained a useful ambiguity, under cover of which the Commons came to be regarded more and more as an essential element. Thus the great list of grievances which was drawn up in the parliament at Stamford in 1309 was said to be presented by 'the good people of the realm assembled in parliament'. We know that the Commons were present in this parliament. We cannot be sure whether they took part in the drawing up of this 'grand remonstrance', but at least we can say that the magnates considered it good politics to put forward their demands in the name of the whole people.

Two years later, in 1311, the baronial committee known as the Ordainers put forward their proposals for the reform of the government. Every clause asserts the authority of parliament. No gifts may be made by the king or new customs levied without the consent of the barons in parliament. The king's chief officers are to be appointed by the barons and to take their oath in parliament. The king is not to go to war without the consent of the barons in parliament. Parliaments are to be held once, and, if necessary, twice a year, for the determination of pleas. The emphasis, it is true, is everywhere on the barons in parliament and the Commons are never mentioned. In actual fact, the Commons were present in every parliament after 1311. Everything that the barons claimed for parliament, in which they were certainly still the dominant element, would in course of time accrue to the Commons.

When the rebel barons were defeated at Boroughbridge, the 'parliamentary' régime they had tried to establish was overthrown. Nevertheless, their insistence on parliament as the ultimate political authority was not in vain. The Statute of York, by which the Ordinances were repealed and the authority of the Crown was re-established, expressly gave to parliament a paramount place in the constitution. It declared that 'the matters which are to be established for the estate of our lord the king and of his heirs, and for the estate of the realm and of the people, shall be treated, accorded and established in parliaments, by our lord the king and by the assent of the prelates, earls and barons, and the community of the realm; according as it hath been heretofore accustomed'. The concluding phrase makes it clear that no revolutionary doctrine is implied. All that is being affirmed is that the proper expression of the will of the community is in parliament. But since the Commons are in fact now regularly summoned to parliaments, they will, nominally at least, participate in whatever parliament does.

But the concurrence of the Commons in parliament was already something more than a formality. This was made clear in the proceedings for the deposition of Edward II and the new settlement. It may well be that the driving force was baronial, but the value of the support of the Commons is shown by the unusual length of their session on that occasion – seven weeks as against the usual two or three.

That the position of the Commons was steadily improving during the reign of Edward II seems clear. Equally clearly their position is still that of subordinates. It might be useful to enlist them on one side or the other in the struggle between king and barons, but of independent activity there is little evidence. Was their attendance at Westminster then merely a convenient source of support for their superiors – were there no advantages to be gained for themselves?

Edward I's great contribution to constitutional history is usually reckoned that he first summoned the Commons to parliament as a normal procedure and not as a purely revolutionary expedient. Great though the importance of the innovation was, it could hardly have been of such consequence had he not also introduced a new conception of law-making.

PETITION AND BILL

LAW originated as unwritten custom and as such was regarded as not susceptible of change. Typical of this early phase is the famous declaration of the barons at Merton in 1236, when they were asked to change the law of bastardy: *Nolumus leges Angliae mutari.* Later it came to be recognized that law could be declared by the general agreement of the feudal council, by 'assize', and the great legal re-organization of Henry II was effected by this process. Even so assize was regarded less as a method of altering the law than of clarifying existing law, and its use was normally administrative. Such were the assizes relating to money and the price of lampreys in the reign of John.

Edward I's innovation consisted in the substitution of the method of petition and grant for the agreement of the assize. This method was based on the immemorial prerogative power of kings to give redress which cannot be got in the ordinary course of law. Edward I was willing to give the prerogative power the widest possible extension: 'In many cases the Lord King on behalf of the common advantage and in virtue of his prerogative is above the laws and customs used in his kingdom.' It is not difficult to see the legislative potentiality of the prerogative interpreted in this way. The grant of a favour to an individual or of rights to a community, for example a county, would create something like a private act of parliament; the granting of a petition from all the communities would make what we now call a public act.

The proper time for presenting these petitions was at the time of parliament, and the first preliminary to the holding of a parliament was the proclamation 'in the Great Hall at Westminster, in the chancery, before the justices of the

bench and in Westcheap, that all those who have petitions
to deliver to us and our council at our forthcoming parliament shall deliver them day by day to those who are assigned
to receive them'. The answering of these petitions became a
large part of the work of the king and council at the time of
parliament. In the well-known words of Fleta: 'The king
has his court in his council, in his parliaments, in the presence of the prelates, earls, barons, lords and others learned
in the law, where doubts about sentences are determined,
where new remedies are provided for new injuries that have
happened, and where justice is meted out to each according
to his deserts.'

As a consequence partly of the new and expanding conception of the prerogative, and partly no doubt of the
presence of the representatives of the Commons in parliament, the volume of petitions to the king greatly increased
in the reign of Edward I. By 1280 they had become too
numerous for the king and his council to deal with, and in
response to complaints that the multitude of petitions had
caused delay in dealing with them, it was ordained that
they were to be sorted into five bundles. Four bundles were
to be dealt with respectively by the Chancellor, the exchequer, the justices, and the justices of the jewry. The fifth
was to contain only those petitions 'which are so great or so
much of grace that they are to come before the king'.

The great majority of these petitions were from individuals or communities such as the religious houses, the two
universities, boroughs and counties, and asked for relief
from particular injustices or for pure favours. As such they
were for the most part dealt with by the council by being
remitted to the proper courts for decision. But those of a
more general kind resulted in decisions of a legislative
character – in statutes.[1] Thus the grant of the customs in

1. The word *statutum* ('it is decided') suggests the exercise of a prerogative power.

Edward's first parliament was embodied in a statute which was said to be made with the assent of those present in parliament, 'at the instance and request of the merchants'; the Statute of Westminster III (1290) purported to be made 'at the instance of the magnates'; and in his last parliament, in 1307, a petition from the laity against payments abroad by religious houses was enacted as the Statute of Carlisle.

Though the expression 'laity' is wide enough to include the Commons, it seems doubtful whether they were in fact associated with the magnates in the presentation of the petition on which the Statute of Carlisle was based. Nor, as we have seen, can we be sure that they had any part in the preparation of the articles at Stamford in 1309. But from the first parliament of Edward III the independent activity of the Commons became unmistakable.

The first petition clearly recorded as emanating from the Commons as a body – the first Commons public bill, as we should call it in modern terminology – was that of 1327. This petition consisted of forty-one articles, each of which dealt with a different subject matter and would in later times have been a separate bill. Sixteen which dealt with more important matters were embodied in statutes with very little change; twenty-two were such that they could suitably be dealt with by some remedy less formal than statute, e.g. ordinance or letters patent; only three were rejected outright, one as being against the law, one as encroaching on the royal prerogative, one as being against the judgment of the council.

Influence of the Commons on legislation. It was a great advance that the Commons should present their petitions corporately and that genuinely national grievances should be separated from private and local requests. The endorsement of the Commons – the petition was literally endorsed with the

words *soit baillé aux seigneurs* [1] – gave their demands the
authority naturally due to a document which had received
the general approval. But the Commons were still in form
and in fact petitioners, and it lay with the Lords and the
king to allow or to reject the remedies proposed. [2] They
might initiate legislation, but they could hardly deserve to
be called legislators so long as they were unable to control
the final result. Often they had difficulty in getting their
petitions properly dealt with at all, and sometimes, owing to
the pressure of other business, they had to ask the king to
hold another parliament for this purpose. What converted
the Commons into effective legislators was their ability to
refuse the grant of supply until remedy had been provided
for their grievances. So long as the king stood in no need of
their financial support, the Commons had no effective
means of bringing pressure to bear. In times of peace the
royal revenues were sufficient to enable the king to dispense
with the support of the Commons and, for the matter of
that, relieved him of the necessity of calling parliaments at
all. But the continual wars of Edward III compelled him to
have constant resort to parliaments – he held forty-eight in
the fifty years of his reign – and it is due to this fact that in
his reign the Commons began to exert an effective influence
on legislation. From 1340 onwards the comprehensive [3]
Commons petition of the type first found in 1327 became a
regular feature of the parliamentary roll and, what is most
to the point, the Commons began the practice of making the

1. *Let it be sent to the Lords.* This formula is still inscribed on every
Commons bill before it is sent to the Lords.

2. Cf. the form of enacting words which came into use during the
reign of Edward III 'at the request of the Commons and by the assent
of the prelates, earls and barons'.

3. After 1426 the Commons began to embody their requests in a
series of separate petitions each dealing with a different subject – in
accordance with modern practice.

grant of supply conditional upon the redress of their grievances. In that year the Commons attached the list of reforms they desired to the document in which the grant of supply was embodied. In 1348 the Commons went a step further, stipulating that the redress of grievances should actually precede the grant of supply.

This weapon – the ability to refuse supply before redress – powerful though it was, was by no means invincible. There were still possibilities of evading the Commons' insistence. The royal assent, *le roi le veut*, did not automatically give legal force to the remedy asked for. The granted petition had still to be converted into the appropriate form of enactment: statute, ordinance or patent. This was the subject of complaint in 1341 and 1385, and to ensure this result the Commons had repeatedly to ask for the statutes or ordinances of reform to be read in their presence before being engrossed or sealed. In 1401 the Commons had to ask that the petitions which were granted might be enrolled before the justices left the parliament, and in 1406 they successfully requested that certain of their number should be appointed to view the enrolment and engrossing of the acts of the parliament.

Nor was there any guarantee that the statute would precisely embody the remedy asked for. When in 1414 the Commons (in their first petition to be written in English) claimed to be 'as well assentors as petitioners' and asked that no statute based upon a Commons petition should contain any additions to, or diminutions from, the original petition without their assent, they had to be content with the bare assurance that nothing would be enacted which was actually contrary to their requests. To the end of the fifteenth century there are numerous instances of the amendment of Commons petitions by the king and lords without their assent. Such amendments might take the form of a proviso for the royal prerogative, a clearer definition of some provision of the petition, some change in the imposition or disposition of the penalties proposed, the limitation of the duration of the statute, or an alteration of administrative detail. On the other hand, amendments to extend the scope of the bill seem to have required the assent of the Commons. The claim to have their requests, if granted, enacted precisely in the terms in which they were asked was not substantiated until after 1500 when, following the example set by the Crown in drafting long and complicated bills of attainder, the Commons began to draft their bills in the form of the desired statute.

By their successful exploitation of the necessities of kings the Commons steadily improved their control over legislation during the fourteenth century. At the height of Richard II's terror, indeed, the Commons were constrained to grant him the customs for life and, thus disarmed, they were compelled to drop their demands for reform. But, with the restoration of a more constitutional conception of government under Henry IV, the Commons resumed the exercise of their power and in the reigns of the first two Lancastrian kings almost all statutes were based on the petitions of the Commons.

But the success of the Commons was not permanent. With an insouciance which seems incredible to the constitutional historian seeking for a steady growth of parliamentary rights, the Commons themselves threw away the advantages they had won. In 1415, in gratitude for the victory of Agincourt the Commons revived the evil precedent of 1397 and granted the customs on wool and tonnage and poundage for life. Again in 1453 at the close of the Hundred Years War similar grants were made to Henry VI. Thereafter the precedent was regularly followed. Edward IV, Richard III and Henry VII got life grants at or soon after their accession. The result could not but be disastrous. Parliaments became rarer. The rule of annual parliaments, which Henry IV and

Henry V had maintained with fair consistency, was no longer observed and intervals of several years became frequent. Henry VII held only seven parliaments in a reign of twenty-four years and could claim it as a virtue that he held so few. At the same time, the volume of legislation initiated by the Commons steadily declined. After 1450 they get fewer statutes enacted and important bills are sometimes rejected. In the reign of Henry VII almost all important legislation originated from the king and council.

AUTHORITIES FOR CHAPTERS I AND II

CAM, H. M. *The Legislators of Medieval England,* 1945.

CLARKE, M. V. *Medieval Representation and Consent,* 1936.

GRAY, H. L. *Influence of the Commons on Early Legislation,* 1932.

JOLLIFFE, J. E. A. *Constitutional History of Medieval England,* 1947.

MAITLAND, F. W. *Selected Historical Essays,* 1957.

PASQUET. *Essay on the Origins of the House of Commons,* 1925.

PETIT-DUTAILLIS, CH., and LEFEBVRE, G. *Studies and Notes Supplementary to Stubbs' Constitutional History,* 1930.

POLLARD, A. F. *Evolution of Parliament.* 2nd Edition, 1926.

RICHARDSON, H. G., and SAYLES, G. O. 'The King's Ministers in Parliament, 1272–1377.' *English Historical Review,* Vols. XLVI and XLVII, 1931 and 1932.

SAYLES, G. O. *The Mediaeval Foundations of England,* 1948.

STUBBS, W. *Constitutional History of England,* 1875.

WEDGWOOD, J. C. *History of Parliament. Register of the Ministers and of the Members of Both Houses, 1439–1509,* 1938.

WILKINSON, B. *Studies in the Constitutional History of the 13th and 14th Centuries,* 1937.

CHAPTER III

LIBERTY OUT OF TYRANNY

Sweet is the name of Liberty, but the thing itself a value beyond all
estimable treasure.   PETER WENTWORTH

ABSOLUTISM, despotism, tyranny – these are the terms in
which the rule of the Tudor kings and queens has often been
characterized. Nor need we dispute that there is ample
justification for such descriptions in the facts. Seldom
has the personal will of the Sovereign counted for so much
in government. And yet the sixteenth century is one of the
most important for the development of the liberties of the
Commons. How is this paradox to be explained?

In the preceding chapter we referred to the success of the
Commons in the early Lancastrian period in getting their
petitions turned into statutes. This fact, combined with the
boldness of their attacks on the government, has encouraged
the view that the early fifteenth century was a golden age of
parliamentary government. 'Never before and never again
for more than two hundred years were the Commons so
strong as they were under Henry IV' wrote Bishop Stubbs
in his classic summary of the reign. Seventeenth-century
lawyers searching for ammunition in their struggle for parliamentary liberties found, or thought they found, many a
precedent for their claims in the records of this period. And
at least one modern constitutional historian has characterized it as one of 'premature constitutional government'.[1]
But a closer examination seems to show that the liberties
of the Commons in this period were far from clearly defined.
Certainly the claim to freedom of discussion was something
less than the modern privilege.

1. G. B. Adams, *Constitutional History of England*, Chapter IX.

FREEDOM OF SPEECH

We have already referred (at the end of Chapter I) to the
procedure at the opening of parliament, which was already
customary in the early fourteenth century and was substantially that followed to-day. The king, usually through the
mouth of the Chancellor, declared the cause of summons to
the whole assembled parliament and then ordered the magnates and the Commons to withdraw to different chambers
to discuss the business laid before them. This procedure
implies at least the possibility of free discussion by the
Commons in the unofficial atmosphere of a private meeting,
and the practice, begun in 1376, of electing a Speaker to
carry their agreed reply to the king goes to confirm this
inference. It is not until the end of the century that we
find the first express claim made for the liberties of the
Commons. In 1397 the Lords, at the instigation of Richard
II, convicted Thomas Haxey of treason for introducing in
the Commons a bill of reforms obnoxious to the king. In
Henry IV's first parliament, the Commons asked that this
judgment be reversed on the ground that it was 'against
right and the course which had been usual in parliament
in violation of the customs of the Commons', and this petition was granted. Haxey was not one of the Commons – he
was a royal official who only introduced, or perhaps drafted,
the bill – and we cannot therefore regard the Commons'
claim as a technical assertion of the right of freedom of discussion. Nevertheless, it was an important affirmation of the
principle that the proceedings of the Commons should be
immune.

Sir Thomas Savage doubtless had Haxey's case in mind
when in the next parliament, that of 1401, upon his election as Speaker, he took the opportunity to deliver a dis-
course upon the rights of the Commons. 'When certain
matters were moved among them', he said, 'some of their

body, to please the king and to advance themselves, would inform the king of such matters before the same had been determined and discussed or agreed upon among the said Commons, by which the king might be incensed against them or some of them'. He therefore begged the king to take no notice of any unofficial report of their proceedings. To this the king replied that 'it was his wish that the Commons should deliberate and treat of all matters amongst themselves ... that he would hear no person, nor give him any credit, before such matters were brought before the king by the advice and consent of all the Commons'. The same principle was reaffirmed in connexion with the financial discussions of the Commons in 1407, when the king declared that 'it shall be lawful for the Commons, on their part, to commune together of the state and remedy aforesaid' [sc. of the realm].

The first express claim for liberty of speech in the Commons was made in 1455. Sir Thomas Yonge, one of the knights for the shire and town of Bristol, brought a petition into the Commons complaining that he had been arrested and imprisoned in the Tower, five years previously, 'for matters by him showed in the House ... notwithstanding that by the old liberty and freedom of the Commons of this land had, enjoyed and prescribed, from the time that no mind is, all such persons as for the time being assembled in any parliament for the same Commons, ought to have their freedom to speak and say in the House of their assembly, as to them is thought convenient or reasonable, without any manner of challenge, charge or punition'. This claim has been described as 'unique in the Middle Ages', and it is true that the political circumstances of the moment happened to be favourable to Yonge. Nevertheless, the fact that he could make his claim in these terms and get it allowed is an indication of contemporary feeling in the matter of freedom of speech.

Thus the principle that the discussions of the Commons ought to be privileged was being asserted in the fifteenth century. It had been the custom almost from the very institution of the office for the Speaker, upon his election, to ask the king to take no notice of anything which he, as Speaker, might report derogatory to the Crown and to believe that the Commons desired only that the rights of the Crown should be maintained. But this was not a claim for freedom of speech inside the assembly of the Commons – it was merely a request that the most favourable construction should be put upon their official utterances through the mouth of the Speaker. Thomas More was the first Speaker (1523) to beg the royal indulgence for any untoward expressions by individuals in debate. In his speech before the king he pointed out that in such an assembly as the Commons 'among so many wise men neither is every man wise alike' and asked the king 'to give to all your Commons here assembled your most gracious licence and pardon freely, without doubt of your dreadful displeasure, every man to discharge his conscience, and boldly in everything incident among, declare his advice, and whatsoever happeneth any man to say, it may like your noble Majesty of your inestimable goodness to take all in good part, interpreting every man's words, how uncunningly soever they may be couched, to proceed yet of a good zeal towards the profit of your Realm and honour of your Royal person ...'

More's novel claim was conceded apparently without reservation or comment. The reality of the concession was soon put to the test. Fourteen days later, Cardinal Wolsey, as Chancellor, came down to the Commons and demanded a subsidy of £800,000 for the war with France. The Commons, appalled by the unprecedented amount, after heated debate, decided to send a deputation to ask the king's Highness 'to be content with a more easier sum.' Wolsey would hear no such suggestion – 'he would rather have his tongue plucked out of his head with a pair of pinsons than to move the King to take any less sum'. Returning again to the Commons House he repeated his demand. The Commons were silent, and when he tried to extract an answer from individual members, 'none of them all would give so much as one word, having before agreed, as the custom was, by their Speaker to make answer'. More's reply was courteous but firm. Falling upon his knees, he excused the silence of the House, affirming 'that for them to make answer was neither expedient nor agreeable with the ancient liberty of the House'. As for himself 'except every one of them could put into his one head all their several wits, he alone in so weighty a matter was unmeet to make his Grace answer'. Whereupon the Cardinal departed. The Commons had made good their claim to debate freely among themselves.

A similar petition for freedom of speech was made by Speaker Moyle in 1542 and was allowed by Henry 'with the greatest humanity'. In Elizabeth's reign, the precedent was regularly followed, and by 1565 it had become sufficiently usual to be included in Sir Thomas Smith's account of parliamentary procedure.

In practice, no doubt, the concession of freedom of speech was not in this period as valuable as it might seem. Henry VIII might find it convenient to pretend to the Pope that the discussions in the English Parliament were free and unrestricted and that the Crown had no power to limit their debates or to control the votes of the members but, as we know, Henry had his own methods of controlling the Commons and could well afford to tolerate the forms of liberty.

Elizabeth frequently warned the Commons off the discussion of certain subjects, particularly religion, trade and the succession. In 1576, Peter Wentworth, the Member for Tregony, made his famous speech. 'In the last and preceding session I saw the liberty of free speech ... so much and so many ways infringed ... Without this it is a scorn and mockery to call it a parliament house.' Alarmed by the boldness of these remarks and much more in the same vein, the House itself took action against Wentworth and committed him to the Tower, whence he was only released a month later at the instance of the queen and after apology and reprimand from the Speaker. Again in the Parliament of 1592–3, when the Speaker made his usual request for liberty of speech, the Lord Keeper's reply shows plainly how the queen conceived the Commons' privilege.

For liberty of speech her majesty commandeth me to tell you, that to say yea or no to bills, God forbid that any man should be restrained or afraid to answer according to his best liking, with some short declaration of his reason therein, and therein to have a free voice, which is the very true liberty of the house, not as some suppose to speak there of all causes as him listeth, and to frame a form of religion, or a state of Government as to their idle brains shall seem meetest, She sayeth no king fit for his state will suffer such absurdities.

The claim to freedom of speech was not finally substantiated in practice until the constitutional struggle of the sixteenth century had been won by parliament. James I went much further than Elizabeth in 1621, when he wrote to Mr Speaker commanding him 'to make known in our name unto the House, that none therein shall presume henceforth to meddle with anything concerning our Government or deep matters of State'. In reply the Commons made the famous Protestation which was afterwards torn out of the Journals by the king's own hand:

That the liberties, franchises, privileges and jurisdictions of Parliament are the ancient and undoubted birthright and inheritance of the subjects of England: And that the arduous and urgent affairs concerning the King, State and defence of the realm, and of the Church of England, and the maintenance and making of laws, and redress of mischiefs and grievances, which daily happen within this realm, are proper subjects and matter of counsel and debate in Parliament: And that in the handling and proceeding of those businesses every member of the House of Parliament hath, and of right ought to have, freedom of speech to propound, treat, reason and bring to conclusion the same ...

In the reign of Charles I the struggle for freedom of speech was merged in the greater conflict between king and parliament. By 1642 when Charles burst into the House of Commons and tried to arrest the Five Members, much more was involved than the formal privileges of the Commons; the issue then was whether government should be with or without parliament. After the Restoration the main constitutional issue was settled, and no attack was made on the privileges of parliament.

Freedom of speech received statutory confirmation after the Revolution of 1688. The Bill of Rights declared 'That the freedom of speech, and debates on proceedings in Parliament, ought not to be impeached or questioned in any court or place out of Parliament.' Thus freedom of speech was finally established.

FREEDOM FROM ARREST

In modern times the privilege of freedom from arrest is not of great value, since it applies only to civil process and imprisonment in civil process has been practically abolished. But it is of historical importance, since it was in connexion with it that the Commons first gained the right to determine and enforce matters of privilege. Before the Tudor period questions of privilege were decided by the king and the Lords.

The privilege of freedom from arrest originated in the ancient protection afforded by the king to persons travelling to and from his court. When the Commons began to come to parliament, this protection was extended to them in virtue of the royal writ of summons. By a natural development protection from molestation was interpreted to mean that persons should not be hindered by arrest from coming to parliament. Early in the fifteenth century the Commons began to claim freedom from arrest except for treason, felony or breach of the peace, but the king and the Lords, though willing to release a particular individual at the request of the Commons as a matter of grace, would not concede any right. Similarly, when Thomas Thorpe, Speaker of the Commons in 1453-4, was imprisoned by order of the court of the Exchequer for not paying a fine, the judges, while recognizing the principle of freedom from arrest, ruled that 'determination and knowledge of that Privilege belongeth to the Lords of the Parliament and not to the justices'.

It was not in fact until the reign of Henry VIII that the Commons gained the right to determine and enforce matters of privilege. Hitherto the Commons had been obliged to petition for a writ out of Chancery in order to obtain the release of an arrested member. But in 1543, when George Ferrers, burgess for Plymouth, was arrested for debt during the time of parliament and the Commons took the matter up to the Lords, they 'judging the contempt to be very great, referred the punishment thereof to the order of the Common House'. The Commons proceeded to order their Serjeant to require delivery of the burgess without any writ or warrant, and when the Lord Chancellor offered to grant a writ they refused it, 'being in a clear opinion that all commandments and other acts of proceeding from the Nether House were to be done and executed by their Serjeant without writ, only by show of his mace, which was his warrant'. After a scuffle in which the mace was broken Ferrers was released. The sheriffs, as the officers responsible for the arrest, were ordered to appear before the Speaker in the Commons and committed to the Tower, whence they were released after two days 'not without humble suit made by the Mayor of London'. The sequel is remarkable for its indication of the king's interest in maintaining the privileges of the House. When the king heard of this proceeding he sent for the Chancellor, the judges, the Speaker and other important members of the lower House and commended them for maintaining the privileges of their House, saying that even their cooks and horsekeepers were free from arrest. Henry is reported to have continued: 'And further we be informed by our judges that we at no time stand so highly in our estate royal, as in the time of Parliament; wherein we as head, and you as Members, are conjoined and knit together into one body politic, so as whatsoever offence or injury during that time is offered to the meanest member of the House is to be judged as done against our person and the whole court of Parliament. Which prerogative of the Court is so great ... as all acts and processes coming out of any other inferior courts must for the time cease and give place to the highest.'

By the end of the sixteenth century the modern principle had become established that the Commons should determine all matters of privilege relating to their House.

THE POWER TO COMMIT

THE power of commitment has been described as the keystone of parliamentary privilege, because it is the means by which the House of Commons punishes all those offences against itself which are now very loosely called 'breaches of privilege', but which formerly were called 'contempts'.

The power to commit had always belonged to the Lords, who as the highest court of record could and can fine, imprison and take security for good behaviour. The Commons on the other hand, as 'newcomers to Parliament' did not inherit the Lords' power as a court and in the mediaeval period specifically rejected a share in the judicial function of parliament. But in the Tudor period their growing sense of their own importance and the recognition of the need of powers to protect their dignity, if not their independence, induced the Commons to make a similar claim to be a court of record. The earliest instances of the use of the power to commit (in the case of Story in 1548, and of Copley in 1558) seem to show more concern to punish disrespect to the Crown than that to their own body. But in 1581, the Commons proceeded against Arthur Hall, the burgess for Grantham, for publishing a book 'not only greatly reproachful against some particular good members of this House, but also very much slanderous and derogatory to the general authority, power and state of this House ... charging this House with drunkenness'.[1] On two earlier occasions Hall had been ordered to appear at the bar of the House 'for sundry lewd speeches' and had got off with an apology and a reprimand from the Speaker. He was now expelled from the House, fined 500 marks and sent to the Tower. Nor were the Commons content merely to discipline their own members. In 1585, they summoned to the bar of the House a currier named Bland for contemptuous words used against the House and released him upon his making his submission and paying 20s. costs. Similar instances of the Commons' claim to be a court of record are frequent in the reign of Elizabeth, but since the middle of the seventeenth century the Commons have virtually, if not in theory, abandoned the claim to impose fines and have restricted their claim to imprison to the period of the session. Committal for the period of the session remains in modern times the most serious penalty which the House can inflict on its own members or other persons who have offended against its rights or dignity.

1. Cf. the resolution of the House in the case of Mr Allighan, 30 October 1947.

CHAPTER IV

RULES, CLERKS, RECORDS

Nothing tended more to throw power into the hands of Administration, and those who acted with the majority of the House of Commons, than a neglect of, or departure from, these rules. ... The forms of proceeding, as instituted by our ancestors, operated as a check and control on the actions of Ministers; and they were in many instances a shelter and protection to the minority against the attempts of power.

SPEAKER ONSLOW

Our parliamentary procedure is nothing but a mass of conventional law.

DICEY

EARLY HISTORY OF PROCEDURE

CERTAIN conditions are necessary before a deliberative assembly can work effectively. The privileges of the Commons, of which some account was given in the last chapter, established those conditions. By their privilege the Commons secured their independence, their right to regulate their own procedure, and the right to discipline offenders against their rights. The present chapter deals with the way in which the House regulated its own procedure.

That there must have been some rules of procedure from the earliest times is obvious, but since the Journals of the Lords do not begin till the reign of Henry VIII and those of the Commons till that of Edward VI, we know practically nothing of the way either House conducted itself before the sixteenth century. An anonymous chronicle tells us that in 1376 members of the Commons made their speeches standing at a lectern in the Abbey Chapter House. In the Lords in 1461 we learn that bills were read two and sometimes three times. The burgesses for Colchester have left on record some details of the proceedings at the opening of parliament in 1485. While king and Lords heard the mass of the Holy Ghost in Westminster Abbey, the names of the Commons were called over by the Lord Steward in the parliament chamber; and the ceremonies at the election of the Speaker had already taken shape.

Rules of Debate. The earliest account of procedure in the House of Commons is that of Sir Thomas Smith, written in 1562-6.[1] This account shows that already the rules of debate had been formulated very much as they are to-day. 'He that standeth up bareheaded is understood that he will speak to the bill. If more stand up, who that first is judged to arise is first heard.' The member in possession of the House is to proceed without interruption: 'with perpetual oration, not with altercation, he goes through till he do make an end'. The modern rule that a member may only speak once to the same question is foreshadowed: 'he that once hath spoken in a bill, though he be confuted straight, that day may not reply; not though he would change his opinion ... for else one or two with altercation would spend all the time'. The House must not be addressed directly: 'every man speaketh as to the Speaker, not as one to another, for that is against the order of the House. It is also taken against the order to name him whom ye do confute but by circumlocution, as "He that speaketh with the bill", or "He that spake against the bill and gave this and this reason" '. 'No reviling or nipping words must be used', and the rule that a member must not 'utter treasonable or seditious words or use the King's name irreverently' is already laid down.

1. Smith's description of Commons procedure is only a part of his book *De Republica Anglorum*. The first treatise devoted solely to Commons procedure is that which William Lambarde (M.P. in 1562–3 and 1566) finished not earlier than 1586.

Method of Voting. Sir Thomas Smith describes the method of voting on a bill as follows: The Speaker 'holdeth the bill up in his hand and sayeth, "as many as will have this bill go forward, which is concerning such a matter, say yea". Then they which allow the bill cry yea, and as many as will not, say no: as the cry of yea or no is bigger, so the bill is allowed or dashed. If it be a doubt which cry is the bigger, they divide the House, the Speaker saying, "as many as do allow the bill go down with the bill, and as many as do not sit still". So they divide themselves, and being so divided they are numbered who make the more part, and so the bill doth speed.' The earliest reference to a division occurs in a letter dated March 26, 1532, and the first to be officially recorded is of the year 1553–4. The method of taking a division remained unaltered until 1836 when, in order to make possible an official record of the names of those voting, the modern procedure whereby both sides go out of the Chamber into separate lobbies was introduced.

Procedure on Motions. The elementary principle that not more than one question should be before the House at a time was implied in 1604 when it was held to be irregular for a member to interpose a motion before a former question was disposed of. The rule was more exactly stated by Scobell, who was Clerk of the House from 1649 to 1659: 'When a Motion hath been made, that Matter must receive a determination by a Question, or be laid aside by the general sense of the House before another be entertained.' Similarly the principle that nothing should be decided without the putting of a question was affirmed in 1614: 'That nothing do pass, by Order of the House, without a Question, and that no Order [*sc.* be made] without a Question Affirmative and Negative.' According to Hatsell, who wrote in 1776, the framing of the question was anciently left to the Speaker. This practice was obviously open to abuse and in

Hatsell's time it had long been obsolete. Speaker Lenthall (1640–60) was criticized as being 'often much confused in collecting the sense of the House and drawing the debates to a fair Question', and Clarendon boasted that as chairman of Committee of the whole House he served the king by 'entangling' the Committee in contradictory motions. As late as 1697 we find the Speaker declaring the sense of the House without putting any question, but already such a proceeding was so unusual as to merit a special entry in the Journal.

The modern rules which require that notice should be given of important questions were not made until later, but provision was made to ensure that the House should not suddenly be confronted with a question by the rule that 'When a motion hath been made, the same may not be put to the question until it be debated, or at least have been seconded or presented by one or more persons standing up in their places.'

Procedure on Bills. As has already been stated, the practice of reading bills three times is found in the Lords in the fifteenth century. After 1509, when the Lords Journals begin, we know that it was the rule. When the Commons Journals begin, in 1547, we find that bills usually received several readings, and down to 1589 as many as four are not uncommon. Occasionally there were as many as six, and, at least once, eight.

Sir Thomas Smith describes the procedure on public bills in the middle of the sixteenth century as follows:

All bills be thrice, on three divers days, read and disputed upon, before they come to the question ... After the bill hath been twice read, and then engrossed, and eftsoons read and disputed upon enough as is thought, the speaker asketh if they will go to the question ... [Here follows the description of a division quoted above] ... It chanceth sometimes that some part of the bill is allowed, some other part hath much doubt and contrariety made of it: and it is thought if it were amended it

would go forward. Then they choose certain committees [1] of them who
have spoken with the bill and against it to amend it and bring it in
again so amended, as they amongst them shall think meet: and this is
before it is engrossed, yea and some time after. But the agreement of
these committees is no prejudice to the House. For at the last question
they will either accept it or dash it as it shall seem good, notwithstanding that whatsoever the committees have done.

Already at this early stage the main outlines of the modern
procedure have been drawn – three readings and committal.
But there are differences. Debate occurs at all three readings and only one question, 'That this bill go forward', is
expressly mentioned. Committal, it is to be noted, was necessary only if the bill was thought to require amendment.

In the seventeenth century procedure developed and became more formal. The three readings gradually became
more like stages in the modern sense. Their purpose was
still mainly informative – the Speaker explained the bill
with the assistance of a brief, which by the middle of the
century had to be presented by a member with the bill.
But whereas in Sir Thomas Smith's time a single question
may have sufficed, in this period a definite question came to
be necessary at each stage. This question, however, was not
as in the modern practice, 'That the bill be now read a
second (or the third) time' but followed the debate and took
the form, 'That the bill be read on a future day'. This tendency to multiply the number of possible questions during
the progress of a bill was carried still further in the eighteenth century and by the middle of the nineteenth century
there might be as many as eighteen questions on a bill – not
counting amendments.

Early Examples of Committee Procedure. The principle of the
committee is almost as old as parliament itself. Any large

1. In the sixteenth and seventeenth centuries 'committee' meant a
member of a committee, not the whole body.

deliberative assembly inevitably delegates the more detailed
and less important work to a smaller body. The receivers
and triers of petitions which began to be appointed in the
reign of Edward I might be regarded as the earliest examples
of the committee principle. And from the moment when
the Commons began to act collectively, committees were
regularly appointed as, for example, to oversee the drawing
up of statutes to carry their petitions into force. Sometimes
joint committees of Lords and Commons were appointed
for this purpose or to audit the accounts of a subsidy.

Committal of Bills. Though we cannot refuse to regard
these as genuine expressions of the committee principle,
their significance is antiquarian rather than historical. The
continuous history of the modern committees of the House of
Commons cannot be traced back earlier than the middle of
the sixteenth century, though their existence before that
period seems certain. We have already quoted the passage
in which Sir Thomas Smith describes the committal of a
bill after second reading, and the Journals, when they begin,
frequently refer to the committal of bills, but, as the Clerk
did not at this period trouble to minute the appointment of
committees in detail, we cannot say much about them. At
this early period, as has already been noted, committal was
by no means the rule, but in the reign of Elizabeth, committal had become the practice for all public bills except
those originating in the Lords. The first detailed entry in
the Journals recording the committal of a bill appears in
1571:

The bill concerning coming to the Church and Receiving of the Com-
munion. – The second Reading; and, after sundry Motions, committed
unto Sir *Thom. Smythe*, Sir *Owen Hopton*, Sir *Thom. Scotte*, the Masters of
the Requests, Mr Servient *Manwood*, Mr Servient *Geffrey*, Mr *Fleetwood*,
and Mr *Sands*; to meet in the Star-chamber To-morrow, at Three of the
Clock in the Afternoon.

The theory of these committees was that which is preserved in modern British practice rather than that which is found in American and Continental practice. They were entirely subordinate and auxiliary to the House, and not bodies to which the House had delegated any part of its authority. In the words of Hooker: 'When any bill is committed, the committees have not authority to conclude, but only to order, reform, examine and amend the thing committed unto them; and of their doings they must give report to the House again, by whom the bill is to be considered.' Indeed, so far was the House from regarding a committee as in any sense acting on its behalf, that in this period it was the rule to appoint to the committee on a bill only those members who had shown themselves in favour of it.

Committees on Matters. The method of committal appears first in our records in connection with single bills. But it was not long before it was discovered that it might equally usefully be employed for matters. Thus in 1571 a committee of twenty was set up 'for the subsidy', another of thirty-six for 'Matters of Religion', a third of thirteen for 'Motions of Griefs and Petitions', and a fourth of nine to consider the validity of certain borough elections. There was also appointed in this session a business committee of fifteen to arrange the order in which bills were to be considered, but this was considered 'a very rare Precedent', and appears not to have been followed again until 1625.

Standing Committees. From the committee dealing with a specific subject matter it was an easy transition to the 'standing' committee appointed to deal with all matters of the same class throughout the session. The committees for 'Matters of Religion' and of 'Motions of Griefs and Petitions' of 1571, already mentioned, were virtually such. In 1581 a standing committee was appointed to deal with *all* disputed election returns, and in each of the parliaments of 1584,

1585, 1586, 1587 and 1588 a committee was appointed to deal with all matters touching privilege. In 1592 and afterwards, privileges and elections were combined in a single large committee consisting of the Privy Councillors and thirty or more other members, and in 1621 standing committees on trade and on courts of justice were appointed. Thus were established the five standing committees which Scobell speaks of as being regularly appointed in the middle of the seventeenth century.

The use of committees, whether for bills or for matters, was thus well established by the middle of the seventeenth century. Many of the characteristics of committee procedure are already apparent. In particular the rule of the House against speaking twice to the same question seems to have been absent from the beginning. A quorum was fixed at first at one half of the total membership, later at eight. The time and place of first meeting were fixed by the House, but thereafter committees 'may, from time to time, until the Report of their Proceedings be made, adjourn, and alter their Place and Time of meeting, and select such sub-committees from amongst themselves, as they shall find cause, for any particular Purpose or Service, to be assigned by themselves, or the House, upon their Report'. Committees usually met in the afternoon to avoid clashing with the sittings of the House. There is recorded in the Journal of 1605 a complete time-table of committees sitting every day of the week from Monday to Saturday. At first they met in various rooms within or without the Palace of Westminster – the Star Chamber, Mr Treasurer's Chamber, Serjeants' Inn Hall, the Temple, or Lincoln's Inn, and in 1607 we hear of 'the committee chamber'.

Committees of the Whole House. The committees to which we have so far referred were all select committees in the sense that they were smaller bodies chosen from the House, or, as

a member in one of Elizabeth's parliaments said, 'an arti-
ficial body framed out of us who are the general body'.
But this convenient instrument for detailed business, which
is universally employed by all modern assemblies, had
hardly been developed, when it was almost entirely abandoned in favour of committees consisting of the whole
House. This strange result is attributable to several causes.

The small committees of Tudor times had been found a
useful instrument of royal influence. They usually included
some, often all, of the Privy Councillors who were members
of the House, through whom the views of the Court could
be brought to bear on the Commons. The rather casual
method of appointing committees in the House undoubtedly
encouraged this abuse, and complaints were repeatedly
made, notably in 1601, when it was said that those furthest
from the Chair were unable to get their nominees appointed.
To remedy this an order was made by the House in 1621,
allowing all members of the House, whether appointed to
a committee or not, to attend and have voices, that is, to be
as effectively members of the committee as if they had been
appointed.

A second reason for the abandonment of small select committees in favour of committees employing every member
was the desire of members to take part in all matters of
consequence and not to leave them to be settled by the
'Grandees'. This aspect of the matter is made quite clear by
Scobell. 'Some bills of great concernment', he says, 'and
chiefly in bills to impose a tax, or raise money from the
people, are committed to a committee of the whole House;
to the end there may be opportunity for fuller debates, for
that at a committee the members have liberty to speak as
often as they shall see cause, to one question; and that such
bills, being of general concernment, should be most
solemnly proceeded in, and well weighed.'

A third reason, which undoubtedly contributed to the

development of committees of the whole House, was that debate would be less constrained in the absence of the Speaker, who was still distinctly the royal servant. The first bill to be committed to a committee of the whole House was the bill for the preservation of the Union with Scotland, 1607, the bill 'against hostile laws' as it was called. The intention of the new procedure is plainly indicated in the Journal by the significant marginal note: 'Privilege – The King's noticing speeches'. The absence of the Speaker from committees of the whole House was not, however, at first a rule, for we find him on 23rd March, 1609/10 in a committee of the whole House sitting in the Clerk's chair, with the Clerk standing at the back and the 'Moderator' of the committee sitting on a stool beside him. But, by the time of the Long Parliament at any rate, the Speaker regularly left the Chair on the question being put, and a chairman was chosen.

Financial Procedure. It is a peculiar feature of financial procedure in the House of Commons that bills to authorize taxation or expenditure have to be preceded by a preliminary stage in a committee of the whole House. At this preliminary stage resolutions are come to, upon the basis of which a bill is drafted. The bill then goes through the ordinary bill procedure. The principle enshrined in this practice is at least as old as the reign of Elizabeth, when subsidy bills had to be preceded by a motion in the House to grant a subsidy. When this motion had been carried, then (in the words of Lambarde) 'the devise and dealing therein is committed to divers, who agree upon articles which they do bring in to be ordered by the House'. The House then bade the Attorney General draw up the articles in the form of an act, which proceeded like other bills.

In the seventeenth century the Commons made rules for financial procedure. In February, 1668, they resolved that if any motion be made in the House for any public aid or charge upon the people, the consideration and debate thereon ought not presently to be entered upon but adjourned to such further day as the House shall think fit to appoint; and then it ought to be referred to the Committee of the whole House and their opinion to be reported thereupon, before any resolution or vote of the House be resolved therein'. This resolution is now embodied in the Standing Orders of the House. Meanwhile there had come into existence the Committee of Supply (1620) and the Committee of Ways and Means (1641), which were Committees of the whole House to which financial proposals were referred. In the course of the next century the functions of these two committees came to be those which they perform to-day. The Committee of Supply votes the ordinary expenditure of the year, the Estimates. The Committee of Ways and Means authorizes the taxes necessary to cover this expenditure in a series of resolutions upon which the Finance Bill is based.

CLERKS AND JOURNALS

The Clerk of the Parliaments. That there must have been an official responsible for the business of parliaments is obvious, and from the frequent appearance of his name on the record of the early parliaments of Edward I we may perhaps infer that John of Kirby was such. It seems probable that he combined this recurrent duty with the permanent duties of clerk of the council. Certainly Gilbert of Rothbury who succeeded him in 1290 held both offices. His principal duties as parliamentary clerk appear from the records to have been to keep the Rolls of Parliament and to see that they were written up. It is not perhaps without significance that the Rolls of Parliament which survive begin with the parliament of 1290, the year of Rothbury's appointment as a clerk of the council.

In the reign of Edward III the clerk in charge of parliamentary business begins to emerge more distinctly. Henry Edwinstone, the first in this reign, was thanked by the king for the labours 'which he has borne on behalf of us and of all our people in our chancery and in our parliaments of which he has been and still is the clerk'. His duties, moreover, as clerk of the parliament began to assume a new importance. Hitherto, as has already been noted, all petitions were first sorted into bundles by the receivers of petitions, who were normally chancery clerks, for consideration by the appropriate tribunal. In 1327 the Commons began the regular practice of presenting a 'common petition' containing the requests and complaints of the whole community. Such petitions, being in the nature of what we should now call public bills, clearly required different treatment from the mass of private petitions dealt with by the receivers. Hence it became one of the principal duties of the clerk of the parliament to receive these common petitions and bring them before the council. It became his duty also to read the replies to such petitions.

By the end of the fourteenth century the status of the Clerk of the Parliaments had become fairly clearly defined. Though a fresh appointment had to be made for each parliament, it was usual to reappoint the same chancery clerk for several parliaments, and in 1399 a stipend of £40 a year was regularly attached to the job. This clearly implies a certain continuity, but the title 'Clerk of the Parliaments' (*plural*), the style which the Clerk of the House of Lords uses to this day, does not appear until 1510. Nor was the Clerkship of the Parliaments in the fifteenth century so much a career as a stepping stone to higher things. On ceasing to be Clerk of the Parliaments he was regularly promoted to Master of the Rolls and might become a baron or a bishop, or even Lord Chancellor. It was only in the middle of the sixteenth century that the post became completely professionalised. Francis Spelman, who held the post for twenty-three years (1551–74), and his successor Anthony Mason, who also held it for twenty-three years, till 1597, may be regarded as the first professional Clerks of the Parliaments.

The principal duty of the Clerk of the Parliaments, as has been said, was to keep up the roll of the parliament. This record usually begins with a more or less detailed account of the opening proceedings – the proclamation in Westminster Hall, the appointment of receivers and triers of petitions, the Chancellor's speech disclosing the cause of summons and the withdrawal of the Commons for deliberation. But the main bulk of the roll consists of the petitions dealt with in parliament, mostly of a public character but including some from individuals, and the answers to them: *le roi le veut, le roi s'avisera*, or *soit fait comme il est désiré*. It is thus a mixed record, consisting partly of the proceedings of parliament, partly of the documents upon which proceedings were taken.

The Lords Journals. There is no complete record of the proceedings of the House of Lords earlier than 1510, when the printed series of House of Lords Journals begins. But even if fragments of earlier journals had not survived, it would be plain from the formality of the Journals when they begin that the practice of journal writing had long been in use. Fragments survive for the years 1449, 1461 and 1497, and it is probably right to ascribe to John Fawkes, who was Clerk of the Parliaments from 1447 to 1470-1, the credit for having started the Lords Journals. For, like the Commons Journals (*see* below), their inception was purely voluntary, not by any order of the House. Like the Commons Journal too, they included at first notes of speeches as well as the record of things done. Robert Bowyer, who was Clerk of the Parliaments from 1610 to 1622, wrote, 'the clerk doth every day ... write into his rough or scribbled book not only the reading of bills and other proceedings of the house, but so far forth as he can, whatsoever is spoken worthy observation: howbeit into the journal book which is the record he doth in discretion forbear to enter many things spoken, though memorable, yet not necessary nor fit to be registered and left to posterity of record'. There was in fact no official recognition of the Journal until January 1620–1, when the Lords appointed a committee 'to view and examine the Entries of the Journal Book', three years before the Commons took similar action.

Commons Clerks and Journals. There is evidence of a clerk specially assigned to the Commons in our earliest account of the constitution of parliament, the *Modus Tenendi Parliamentum.* If we are correct in assigning this document to a date about 1327 it would accord well with what we know of the corporate activity of the Commons and the emergence of the common petition in the parliament of that year. The first appointment by letters patent of an 'under-clerk of the Parliaments', as the Clerk of the Commons is still styled in his patent, was that of Robert de Melton in 1363. Like his superior, the under-clerk was a chancery clerk, but his emoluments and subsequent career were on a much more modest scale. A hundred shillings a year was the regular salary until 1529, when it was doubled. A living or a prebend, often of St Stephen's Westminster, was the greatest reward which an under-clerk could expect, and until modern times only one instance is known of an under-clerk being knighted – Thomas Haseley. His career (1414–40) was exceptional: he was chosen by Henry V personally, his knighthood was for unparliamentary services, and he is the only Clerk of the period known to have been in prison.

We know little of the duties of Commons Clerks before Tudor times. Robert Ormeston, who was Commons Clerk from 1515 to 1545, is the first known to have kept any kind of record or book. This record was almost certainly not a journal and was probably the book in which the Act of 1515 prescribed that the names of members to whom the House has granted leave of absence were to be entered. Hooker, who was member for Tiverton in 1571, tells us that 'the Speaker has to see that the clerk do enter and make true records, and safely keep the same and all Bills', and that, after the second reading of a bill, the Speaker must 'cause the Clerk to engross the same'.

To John Seymour, who held his appointment for twenty years from the first parliament of Edward VI in 1547, is due to credit of having begun the record which was after-wards to become the Journal of the House of Commons. The compilation of this does not appear to have been any part of his official duties. Beginning it as a mere note of the readings of bills, he gradually expanded it from three pages per session in the first parliament to eleven pages in the last session of Elizabeth's second parliament. As the record pro-ceeds we find, in addition to the stages of bills, notes of roll-calls, orders of the House concerning privilege, and in 1553-4 the first division figures. He also gives us a valuable account of the election of the Speaker and his three requests for privilege: for free speech in the House, freedom from arrest for members and their servants, and access to the king and queen for the members of the House.

Fulke Onslow, Clerk from 1567 to 1602, carried on the work begun by Seymour, with the difference that whereas Seymour's were rough notes Onslow's was a written-up journal. This difference was not entirely an improvement. Onslow's record is the more readable, but it frequently omits important facts – he records no division figures earlier than 1576. Moreover, his attempt to include the substance of speeches, though it makes for interest, is from the technical point of view retrograde. The primary function of the Clerk of the House of Commons is to record its collective *acts* and in particular its votes, not the speeches of individual members. It was not until 1628, however, that this distinction was clearly recognized. In that year, as a result of the king's expressing a desire to see a speech entered in the Journal, the House resolved that 'the entry of the clerk of particular men's speeches was without warrant at all times'. When at a much later date the House sanctioned the reporting of debates, the task was entrusted to a separate staff (*see* pp. 61–2).

The House did not at once recognize the value of the Clerk's Journal, and our earliest reference to its use as an authoritative source of precedent comes from 1580–1, when a precedent was sought for the procedure to be followed upon a vacancy in the Speakership. Onslow was then called upon to read the 'original book of notes'. Indeed we do not find any evidence of the House taking official control of the Journal until February, 1623–4, when it resolved to appoint a committee to 'survey the clerk's Book of Entries every Saturday in the afternoon'.

In the seventeenth century the House took an increasing interest in its forms and precedents, as the numerous resolutions recorded in the Journals testify. In the stormy sessions of the Long Parliament, moreover, rule and order in proceeding acquired a new importance. The result was inevitably to raise the position of Clerk of the House of Commons from that of a merely mechanical recorder and preserver of records to that of an expert and adviser in procedure. Henry Elsying, who was Clerk in the early years of the Long Parliament, was the first Clerk to appear in the role of guardian of procedure. He it was of whom it was said that for 'his abilities and prudence, more reverence was paid to his stool than to the Speaker's chair'. He was succeeded in 1649 by Henry Scobell, whose *Memorials* is the main authority for seventeenth-century procedure. In 1658 Scobell claimed to be Clerk of the 'Other House' which

Cromwell substituted for the Lords (*see* p. 180) and carried off the Commons Journals so that they could not be searched. In this awkward situation the Speaker remarked, 'The clerk is gone, and you could not carry on your business without one.'

John Hatsell, Clerk of the House of Commons from 1768 to 1820, made an elaborate collection of *Precedents of Proceedings in the House of Commons*, which is the best authority for eighteenth-century procedure. Thomas Erskine May, who was Clerk of the House from 1871 to 1886, first published his *Treatise on the Law, Privilege, Proceedings and Usage of Parliament* in 1844. This work, now in its sixteenth edition, is the prime authority on procedure not only at Westminster but in the legislatures of the Commonwealth.

THE PUBLICATION OF PROCEEDINGS AND DEBATES

OF the publication of the proceedings of parliament before the reign of Elizabeth little is known. The publication of Acts of Parliament in the county courts was usual from the very earliest times and was an elementary necessity of government. Similarly the Clerk of the Parliaments was required to provide transcripts of judicial processes on demand at the rate of ten lines a penny. But in the earliest period no trace appears of the attitude of secrecy which afterwards came to characterize the House of Commons in the sixteenth, seventeenth and eighteenth centuries. On the contrary, there is evidence that it was quite usual for members to make a report to their constituents when claiming their wages upon their return from parliament. We hear of such a practice in 1449 when the member for Lyme Regis 'ingeniously related the transaction of Parliament', and in 1523 the representatives of the city of Lincoln made a similar report on what they had done in parliament. How general this practice was and how long it went on we have no means of knowing, but it seems likely that it passed with the practice of paying members, which had become nearly obsolete before the end of the sixteenth century.

Early in the reign of Elizabeth the House of Commons began to adopt a secretive attitude in regard to its proceedings. 'Every person of the Parliament,' says Hooker, 'ought to keep secret and not to disclose the secrets and things done and spoken in the Parliament House to any manner of person, unless he be one of the same House, upon pain to be sequestered out of the House, or otherwise punished as by the order of the House shall be appointed.' In 1589, upon complaint made by Sir Edward Hobby that matters under discussion in the House had become the subject of talk outside, the House ordered Mr Speaker to admonish members not to speak or write of its proceedings to any person not being a member of the House. A stranger found present in the House during its debates was taken into custody by the Serjeant at Arms and not released until he had sworn at the bar of the House not to disclose what he had heard.

It was in the first half of the seventeenth century that the House, with the growing interest in its own procedure which characterizes the period, began to formulate rules in the matter of records and publications. We have referred to the order of the House of 1628 forbidding the clerk to record speeches. The rule was affirmed in 1640, when Mr Rushworth, on his appointment as Clerk Assistant, was ordered not to 'take any notes here without the precedent directions and commands of the House, but only of the orders and reports made in this House'. In 1641 an order was made that 'no member of this House shall either give a copy, or publish in print, anything that he shall speak here without leave of the House', and another ordered members 'to deliver out no copy or notes of anything that is brought into the House, propounded or agitated in the House'. These two orders thus effectively covered the whole field of parliamentary publication: debates and proceedings. At the same time the House ordered that certain of its resolutions should be printed, and the practice of making occasional orders of this kind went on until 1681, when a general order brought into being the *Votes and Proceedings*. This daily record has been published continuously (except in 1702) from that day to this. The total effect of these orders was to establish the principle that nothing relating to the proceedings of the House should be published except by its order. For two centuries the House struggled to maintain this principle against growing evasion.

The *Votes and Proceedings of the House of Commons* contain only the record of the acts of the House, not of the words spoken in debate, and it is worth remarking that the proposal for even this limited amount of publicity was opposed by one member on the ground that it constituted a 'sort of appeal to the people'. But this was a solitary objection. The majority took the opposite point of view. In the words of one member: 'This printing is like plain Englishmen, who are not ashamed of what they do, and the people you represent will have a true account of what you do.'

Although the House thus early made arrangements for the regular publication of its collective acts, it was nearly two centuries before similar arrangements were made for recording the acts of individual members. It was not until 1836 that official Division Lists began to be published regularly – though Burke had recommended it in 1770. Before the nineteenth century such lists had appeared only unofficially in the shape of electioneering material – the earliest example being in 1689.

Publication of Debates – 'Hansard'. The speeches of members are in an entirely different class. Though on occasion the House would order the printing of speeches by leading members, the only records of speeches in Elizabethan times were the private diaries of members, which formed the basis of the journal compiled by d'Ewes fifty years later. Similarly Anchitell Grey took full notes from 1667 to 1694, which were afterwards published as Grey's Debates. Andrew Marvell regularly informed his constituents of the proceedings in the House of Commons from 1660 to 1678. The latter half of the seventeenth century was also the great period of the news-letter writers, whose trade supplied the demand of the county families for news. For the greater part of this period the trade was plied quite openly, and it was not until 1694 that the House began to take objection. In that year one Dyer was brought to the bar of the House and compelled to acknowledge his offence, to ask for pardon and to receive a reprimand from the Speaker 'for his great presumption'.

Dyer's condemnation was followed by a general order 'that no news-letter writers do, in their letters or other papers that they disperse, presume to intermeddle with the debates or any other proceedings of this House'. From this time onward conflicts with reporters were frequent. In 1722 the order against news-letters was extended to printed newspapers and also made to apply to proceedings in committee as well as in the House. In 1738 it was declared a breach of privilege to publish reports either during the session or in the recess. The argument most generally professed in favour of this order was the danger of misrepresentation, but one member argued that even if the unofficial reports did not misrepresent the speeches of members, they ought to be forbidden, because their publication tended to make members responsible for what they had said in the Chamber to persons outside. In 1762 the policy of secrecy was carried to the extreme, when the House threatened to 'proceed with the utmost severity' against offenders. Nine years later, in 1771, Wilkes took up the challenge. At his instigation several printers published reports of debates without the customary precaution of disguising the names of the speakers, and he with Crosby and Oliver, two other members, resisted all attempts to arrest them. Exasperated, the House ordered the three members to appear at the bar. Wilkes refused; Crosby and Oliver obeyed and were committed to the Tower for the rest of the session. Their release was the signal for a great popular demonstration, and their progress from the Tower to the City was a triumphal march. The victory of the reporters had been won. The House formally reaffirmed the publication of debates to be a breach of its privileges, but from this time onward made no attempt to enforce its order.

Official arrangements for reporting the proceedings of the House begin in 1803, when reporters were assigned a bench of their own in the gallery. At this time William Cobbett undertook the reporting of debates, which he continued until 1812, when T. C. Hansard, who gave his name to the series of Parliamentary Debates, took over the job. In 1908 upon a complaint being made of the shortening of back-benchers' speeches a Select Committee recommended the appointment of an official staff of reporters, and since that time a full verbatim record of all speeches has been made and published. At the present time all speeches, whether in the House or in any of the standing committees on bills, are reported and published. The only exceptions are that no record is made of speeches in secret sessions of the House such as are occasionally arranged in time of war, nor when 'strangers are spied'. A select committee usually sits in private, and its proceedings and any evidence given before it remain confidential until they are reported to the House.

CHAPTER V

CONSENT TO TAXATION

They took infinite pains to inculcate as a fundamental principle, that in all monarchies the people must in effect themselves, mediately or immediately, possess the power of granting their own money, or no shadow of liberty could subsist. BURKE

THE CONSENT OF PARLIAMENT TO TAXATION
IS FINALLY ESTABLISHED

In our account of the origin of parliament we stressed the importance of the feudal duty of the vassal to give counsel to his lord. Hardly less important from the point of view of parliamentary origins was the feudal duty of military service. Ever since the Conquest there had been an obligation upon every tenant-in-chief to put a certain number of knights into the field when required. In the course of time this service came to be commuted for the money payment known as scutage. So long as the obligation was discharged by the provision of knights, there could be little dispute as to the occasions when it was due – they would be determined simply by the fact or the imminence of war. But as soon as the military obligation became convertible into a financial one, there was no clear limit to the occasions when it might be exacted. It might be asked for in peace or war at the king's mere discretion. It was this possibility which John exploited to convert the duty of military service into a source of revenue. It was his practice, at least in his later years, to proclaim a campaign, designate certain barons to follow him and to order the Exchequer to collect scutage from the remainder.

One of the main objects of the Great Charter was to check this abuse. The Great Charter laid down that no scutage or aid (except certain customary aids [1]) was henceforth to be imposed except by 'the common counsel of our kingdom' and prescribed the manner in which this 'common counsel' was to be obtained. The bishops, abbots, earls and greater barons were to be summoned individually; other tenants-in-chief were to be summoned collectively through the sheriffs of their counties.

The view that the Great Charter marks a great step forward in constitutional progress has long been discredited. It is now clear beyond a doubt that its main purpose was to state and define existing feudal rights and duties. The importance of the Charter was not that it introduced any new principle, but that it declared, in the most authoritative manner, a principle which was capable of development in parliamentary history. In the course of time it came to mean that no tax might be imposed without the consent of parliament.

It was a slow process, and it was only in the seventeenth century that the principle was finally established. Before that result could be achieved there had to be a long history of parliamentary struggle – Commons protest and royal evasion. The first contest was over the Customs. Edward I reluctantly conceded that the duties on imports and exports should be levied only at the ancient, the 'customary', rate. In 1340, at the petition of the Commons, a statute was enacted that no charge or aid whatsoever should be levied without the consent of parliament, and the right of the Crown to levy the customs was abolished in terms. This act did not, however, prove conclusive. Repeated attempts were made to evade the rule and it was not until the end of the century that it became established in practice.

1. The 'aids of course' were (1) for ransom of the lord, (2) on the occasion of the knighting of his eldest son, and (3) on the marriage of his eldest daughter.

Rarely, if at all, did the Lancastrian kings attempt to raise a direct tax without parliamentary approval.

The Tudors made no attempt directly to challenge the rule of parliamentary consent to taxation – it had been established too long – but they resorted to various extra-parliamentary methods which could not be held directly to violate the law. Such were benevolences and forced loans. Taxes on imports were held not to be taxes on English subjects and therefore not covered by the law of 1340, and it could even be claimed that taxes on exports could be imposed without recourse to parliament, in virtue of the royal prerogative to regulate trade. On the same principle the Crown granted monopolies to individuals for the exclusive sale of commodities. By the end of Elizabeth's reign this abuse had been carried to great lengths. A bill was introduced to abolish the monopolies, and only the queen's promise to put them within the cognizance of the courts prevented it being carried.

It was the elimination of these non-parliamentary methods of raising money which constituted the final establishment of parliament's control of taxation under the first two Stuarts. The story may be briefly told. In 1606 James I imposed an extra duty of 5s. a cwt. on imported currants by an act of prerogative and was upheld by the judges. Shortly afterwards a new 'book of rates' was issued imposing heavy additional duties on many imports. Parliament remonstrated but acquiesced. In James's second parliament (1614) the Commons declared that the king had no right to impose taxes without the consent of parliament and refused supply before redress of grievances. James replied by dissolving parliament and sending four of the Commons to the Tower. There followed an interval of six years during which James contrived to manage without parliament. All the old extra-parliamentary devices, forced loans and benevolences among them, were revived, and a new one, the sale of titles,[1] introduced. At last, in 1620, James was obliged to summon a parliament to provide supplies in case of war against the Spaniards. The Commons, who were sympathetic to the object, granted two subsidies at the beginning of the session of 1621, contrary to their usual practice of withholding supply before redress of grievance. Nevertheless, in this parliament a determined attack was made on one of the forms of extra-parliamentary revenue – the monopolies. A thorough investigation was made into their abuse, and their holders were successfully impeached.

The struggle was carried on against Charles I. In his first two parliaments the Commons asserted their old right to withhold supply before redress of grievances. In 1628, in his third parliament, the Petition of Right received the royal assent. It asked that 'no man hereafter be compelled to make or yield any gift, loan, benevolence, tax or such like charge without common consent by act of parliament'. The Commons granted five subsidies and were preparing to protest against the illegal collection of tonnage and poundage, when they were dissolved. The crisis came in 1635, when Charles converted ship money, a legitimate form of levy upon the port towns in time of war, into a regular source of revenue by imposing it throughout the country. For the moment Charles was successful; John Hampden was condemned by the judges for refusing to pay it, and the levy was collected in the three succeeding years. For eleven years Charles managed without a parliament. But the election of 1640 brought to parliament a House of Commons more determined and unanimous than ever before. Once again, and for the last time, the collection of tonnage and poundage without the consent of parliament was declared to be illegal; ship money, compulsory knighthood and the abuse of the forests were abolished and the royal right of

1. Baronetcies were invented at this time expressly for the purpose of raising money.

purveyance was limited. This statute was re-enacted at the Restoration, along with the other important legislation of this parliament. Parliamentary control of taxation was never challenged again.

THE COMMONS GAIN SOLE CONTROL
OF TAXATION

The Commons alone initiate Taxation. Parliament thus finally destroyed the claim of the Crown to levy taxes without its consent. By that time, too, the Commons had established their supremacy over the Lords in matters of finance. The Commons owed their place in parliament to the necessity of securing their assent to aids. It was the unwillingness of the Lords to take responsibility for raising the subsidy demanded in 1254 which had brought the Commons to Westminster. From the moment of their arrival it was inevitable that the Commons, as the ultimate source of revenue, should eventually become the effective controllers of taxation. During the fourteenth century, indeed, grants were regularly made by the Lords and Commons jointly, but at the end of this period a form appears which indicates the true position of the Commons as the sole originators of taxation. In 1395 the grants were made 'by the Commons with the advice and assent of the Lords', and thereafter this formula was followed with few exceptions. In 1407 the initiative of the Commons was further emphasized by Henry IV, when he conceded that 'any grant by the Commons granted and by the Lords assented to' should be reported to him only in the manner accustomed, that is to say, by the mouth of the Speaker of the Commons. Accordingly the enacting words of a modern money bill begin: 'Most Gracious Sovereign, we, Your Majesty's most dutiful and loyal subjects, the Commons ... have freely and voluntarily resolved to give and grant ...';

and after it has been agreed to by the Lords, such a bill is returned to the Commons in order that it may be carried to the Lords by the Speaker for the Royal Assent.

The position of the Commons as the exclusive originators of taxation was conclusively affirmed in the 1660s when they refused a first reading to a number of Lords bills to impose taxes.

The Lords may not amend Taxation Bills. In the next decade the Commons went beyond the claim to be the sole originators of taxation and began to deny the right of the Lords even to amend a money bill. In 1671 they resolved, 'That in all aids given to the king by the Commons, the rate or tax ought not to be altered by the Lords', and, in 1678, 'that all aids and supplies, and aids to His Majesty in Parliament, are the sole gift of the Commons; and all bills for the granting of any such aids and supplies ought to begin with the Commons; and it is the undoubted and sole right of the Commons to direct, limit and appoint in such bills the ends, purposes, considerations, conditions, limitations, and qualifications of such grants, which ought not to be changed or altered by the House of Lords'. In 1693 the Lords entered a protest in their Journals affirming their right to amend money bills, but from this time onwards the Commons' claim, if not yet formally admitted, had in practice to be conceded. The Commons on their side registered their victory by the practice which they now (1694) began of recording in the Journals the unimportant Lords amendments to money bills which they were willing to allow, 'to the end that the nature of them may appear'.

The Commons' denial of the right of the Lords to amend money bills has from time to time received further confirmation and definition. Broadly the modern rule may be stated as follows. Bills of 'aids and supplies', including the Finance bills, which impose taxation, and Consolidated Fund bills, which authorize expenditure, may not be amended by the Lords in any way whatsoever. Any amendment by the Lords to such a bill, whether it affects a charge or not, is regarded as an intolerable breach of privilege. In the case of all other bills, on the other hand, the Commons claim privilege only in respect of an interference with a charge, and hold themselves free to accept such alterations with no more than a special entry in their Journals explaining the reason for waiving their privilege.

The Lords may not reject Money Bills. The right of the Lords to reject bills, including those imposing a charge, was not affected by the resolutions of 1671 and 1678. In theory, at any rate, they retained the right as one of the Houses of legislature, to reject any bill sent up from the Commons, but in practice they refrained from rejecting bills exclusively concerned with matters of supply and ways and means – until 1860.

Before 1860 it was the practice to impose or repeal separate classes of taxes by means of separate bills, and, as has been said, the Lords refrained in practice from rejecting such bills. In that year, however, they broke away from the tradition and insisted on their technical right to reject the Paper Duties Repeal Bill. To counter this action, the Commons adopted the device of including all the taxation proposals of the year in a single bill. By this means the Lords were presented with the alternatives of either accepting or rejecting the whole of the financial provision for the year, since amendment of such a comprehensive bill had long been acknowledged to be unconstitutional. In the event the device was successful, and the Lords, rather than enter into direct conflict with the Commons, accepted the bill. The same procedure was followed by the Commons in succeeding years with the same success until 1909, when the Lords rejected the Finance Bill.

The story of the Parliament Act, 1911, belongs to Chapter XII, but it will be convenient to summarize its financial provisions here. By that Act a bill which has been certified by the Speaker as relating only to taxation or expenditure must be passed by the Lords without amendment and submitted for the Royal Assent within one month of their receiving it from the Commons. Thus the financial control of the Commons was completed and the Lords were precluded from amending and rejecting not only bills of 'aids and supplies' (e.g. Finance Bills), but any bill which relates exclusively to expenditure (e.g. Consolidated Fund Bills).

AUTHORITIES FOR CHAPTERS III—V

CAMPION, G. F. M. *Introduction to the Procedure of the House of Commons.* 3rd Edition, 1958.

NEALE, J. E. 'The Commons' Privilege of Free Speech in Parliament', *Tudor Studies*, 1924.

NOTESTEIN, W. *The Winning of the Initiative by the House of Commons*, 1924.

PICKTHORN, K. *Early Tudor Government*, 1934.

POLLARD, A. F. Articles on Clerks of Parliament. *Bulletin of the Institute of Historical Research*, 1937–40. *English Historical Review*, 1942.

REDLICH, J. *The Procedure of the House of Commons*, 1908.

STRATEMAN, C. *The Liverpool Tractate*, 1937.

TANNER, J. R. *Tudor Constitutional Documents*, 1922. *English Constitutional Conflicts of the 17th Century*, 1928.

WILLIAMS, O. C. *Officials of the House of Commons*, 1909. *The Clerical Organization of the House of Commons, 1661–1850*, 1954.

CHAPTER VI

THE MINISTRY BECOMES
RESPONSIBLE TO THE COMMONS

Ministers seldom love parliament, never bring business there for counsel, but to carry points that must have the authority of the Legislature; and in order to carry such points must previously strengthen themselves there by collecting all the force they can get for it.

SPEAKER ONSLOW

EARLY ATTEMPTS TO CONTROL POLICY

WE have seen how the Commons from being mere petitioners became legislators in the fourteenth century and how in the seventeenth they established themselves in sole control of taxation. Both of these were great achievements, but neither in itself gave them control of the government. It was something for the Commons to be able to propose and to be required to assent to the laws by which they would be governed, but they had no direct or regular means of ensuring that the law would be properly administered. Nor did the power of the Commons to refuse supply carry the Commons into the heart of government. At best the threat could divert policy on a crucial issue, at worst refusal produced a political deadlock verging on civil strife. It was the task of the eighteenth century to devise the method whereby parliament might exercise a continuous control of policy, or at least get rid of the government it did not like, without resort to violence. This is the method of ministerial responsibility. It consists in the fact that the government is carried on by ministers, who are dependent upon a majority in the lower House and can be changed for other ministers without the constitution itself being overthrown. Many refinements and conventions are necessary to ensure the smooth working of this system – but, in essence, it depends on the power of the Commons to change the ministry.

The right of the magnates to be consulted on matters of policy was rooted in feudal theory. They were the king's 'natural counsellors' and, as we have seen, it was failure to consult them on foreign policy which led to the original demand for 'parliament'. Henry III's few expeditions were made with the support of parliament and Edward I never engaged in war without obtaining advice – and aid – from a parliament. The right of parliament to decide questions of peace and war was one of the demands of the Ordainers, and the earls who refused to fight for Edward II at Bannockburn were exercising this right. In the later years of Edward II the chief purpose of summoning parliaments was the proposed expedition to France.

The Commons had no such original status as counsellors. They had come to parliament as assentors to a demand for financial assistance. When they are first consulted on matters of policy, their participation is always closely connected with their financial role. In 1328, a treaty of peace with Scotland was said to be concluded with the counsel and consent of the prelates, earls, barons and Commons. From the beginning of the Hundred Years War the Commons were frequently asked for their advice. In 1343, the Lord Chamberlain told parliament that 'as the war was begun by the common advice of the prelates, great men and Commons the king could not treat of, or make, peace without the like assent', whereupon the Lords and Commons, after separate deliberation, gave their separate answers.

The Commons were not, however, eager to claim a share in policy. When they were asked for their advice on peace or war in 1348, they excused themselves on the ground of their 'ignorance and simplicity', undertaking to accept whatever the king and magnates should ordain. In 1384, when Richard II pressed them for a plain answer to a similar question, they protested in terms that they should not be charged as counsellors nor be understood to advise one way or the other.

During the Wars of the Roses parliament ceased to be an instrument of national policy in any true sense and became a mere machine for registering the alternate victories of the rival factions. With the cessation of civil strife, in the reign of Henry VII, parliament once more resumed its old attitude to questions of peace and war. But the context is still financial. Henry VII's few parliaments were all summoned with a financial purpose, and if it was his invariable practice to consult parliament on the expediency of his wars, that was only because its financial support was necessary. To the extent that he was under the same necessity, Henry VIII was obliged to seek the concurrence of the Commons in his foreign policy, and Wolsey's famous intrusion into the Commons was prompted by the need of funds for the war with France. But so long as other non-parliamentary methods of raising money were open to the king, parliament could never achieve a continuous or decisive voice in foreign policy – still less in any other matter of policy, unless it required legislation. It was not, in fact, until the Commons had won the sole right to impose taxation that they could begin to establish their position as critics and controllers of policy.

It has been well said that the Restoration was 'a restoration of Parliament, even more than a restoration of the king'.[1] For if, outwardly, the position of the Crown was the same, the realities of power were very different. 'The Civil War had reversed the relation between Whitehall and Westminster; the members now feared nothing from the Court, but courtiers feared much from Parliament.'[2]

1. S. R. Gardiner, *Student's History of England*, 1890–1, p. 580.
2. G. M. Trevelyan, *England under the Stuarts*, 1904, p. 375.

Essentially, this change in the balance of power within the constitution was due simply to the discovery that a king could be defeated in battle and that without an armed force he could not in the long run resist the will of parliament. Technically, the victory of parliament consisted in the fact that at the Restoration the claim to levy taxes without the consent of parliament was finally abandoned. From this time forward no attempt was made to evade the financial control of parliament through benevolences or forced loans.

While the destruction of absolute power is one thing, the effective control of policy is quite another, and the process by which this was achieved took more than a century and a half to complete.

Refusal of Supply. It is often said that the power of the Commons to control the executive is based on their power to withhold supplies. In the long run doubtless this is true. But the refusal of supply could hardly be the normal method of enforcing control. Indeed, it would be most unfortunate if it were. The birch may be the ultimate sanction for authority in a school, but a state of affairs in which it is constantly in use can hardly be regarded as satisfactory. Nor does a constitution work well in which the legislature resorts frequently to the threat to refuse supply. In actual fact in the early stages, when the Commons were still groping for methods of controlling policy, they were not able to employ the financial weapon effectively. Their first act after the Restoration was to grant Charles an income sufficient for the ordinary purposes of government for life – estimated at £1,200,000. A similar, in fact a more favourable, financial arrangement, calculated to produce £1,900,000, was made for James. Consequently, in these two reigns the Commons deprived themselves of the weapon which they might have used to bring pressure to bear on royal policy, at least in time of peace. During the earlier part of his reign, Charles was quite willing to take the Houses into his confidence in matters of foreign policy and to listen to the advice they offered in the form of Addresses. But in 1677 Charles refused to comply with the request of the Houses to make an alliance with the Dutch, whereupon the Commons threatened to withhold supplies. To this the king objected that if he were to allow 'this fundamental power of making peace and war to be so far invaded … as to have the manner and circumstance of leagues prescribed to me by Parliament, it is plain that no prince or state would any longer believe that the sovereignty of England rests in the Crown'. Nevertheless, he was obliged to yield, treaties were made, and the Commons thanked him and voted supplies.

For the moment, the threat of refusing supply appeared to be effective. When, however, it came to the approval of the alliance, Charles, though willing to lay the text of the treaties before the Houses, refused to disclose the relevant diplomatic correspondence. Thereupon, the Commons presented an Address requesting the removal of the counsellors who advised the treaties. But Charles was already receiving a pension of £100,000 a year from the King of France as the price of peace, and he could afford to ignore the protests of the Commons. Without further discussion, he prorogued parliament, merely remarking that he had been very ill used by the Commons.

Impeachment. In these circumstances, the Commons sought some more effective method than that of protest and Address for bringing royal advisers to account. At the next crisis in the quarrel over foreign policy the Commons resorted to the ancient weapon of impeachment. In 1677, the Commons, incensed by the discovery of the secret treaty with the King of France, impeached the Earl of Danby, the minister who had negotiated it. Though the process was never completed and a bill of attainder was rejected by the Lords, the Commons achieved their purpose. Danby was dismissed from the office of Lord Treasurer and committed to the Tower.

Although, as we have seen, parliamentary control of policy in the Middle Ages was confined to questions of peace and war and could be exercised only through its power to refuse supply, the problem of controlling royal ministers had arisen in another context, namely the conduct of administration. In the thirteenth century, the magnates had produced many schemes for bringing the royal advisers under control, but all had failed through lack of a mechanism whereby ministers could be made answerable to parliament. The Commons, when they became active in parliament, were faced with the same difficulty. In 1341, under the threat of refusing supply, they obtained a statute which required that ministers and judges should be bound to surrender their offices at the next parliament and be then responsible to all having cause of complaint against them. It was a gallant attempt to secure something like ministerial responsibility, but it broke down because the ministers and judges refused to serve on these terms. Under the conditions of fourteenth-century monarchy it was not possible for a minister to conceive of himself as owing loyalty to any but the king, and the attempt to introduce responsibility to parliament was not made again.

In exceptional circumstances the Commons could remove a royal minister of whom they disapproved by impeachment – a judicial process in which the Commons acted as accusers before the Lords as judges. Thus, during the temporary ascendancy which they enjoyed in the Good Parliament of 1376, the Commons had been able to clinch their demand for administrative reform by securing the condemnation and arrest of the ministers whom they held responsible. But it was soon discovered that this weapon could equally well be used by the king against his enemies – it was little use to the Commons so long as the Lords supported the king – and the process was soon abandoned.

With the sole exception of the proceedings against the Duke of Suffolk in 1450, the right of impeaching ministers lay dormant for two centuries. It was revived against Mompesson in 1621 for abuse of monopolies – a charge only indirectly political. But the impeachment of Sir Francis Bacon, Chancellor in the same year, though in form for accepting bribes in his court was certainly inspired by hostility to the royal policy, for which he was held responsible. In 1640, the Earl of Strafford was impeached expressly for his political conduct. The full significance of impeachment as a stage in the history of ministerial responsibility became clear in the case of Danby. In impeaching him the Commons were aware that he had acted only upon the king's orders, but it was established that the king's written order could not be pleaded in defence and that a royal pardon could not avail to stop the trial. These decisions it was which fully converted impeachment into an instrument for enforcing ministerial responsibility. Though the process of impeachment itself was abandoned as a political instrument almost as soon as it had been perfected,[1] its immediate contemporary value was that it made possible an attack on the royal policy without recourse to rebellion. To the modern constitution the principle is fundamental. It means that ministries may come and go, but the king's business, the government of the country, goes on.

1. The last instance of its purely political use was in 1713, when the Tory ministers were impeached for their share in the Treaty of Utrecht. The last two impeachments were those of Warren Hastings in 1788 on charges of misgovernment in India, and of Lord Melville in 1806 for malversation of public funds while in office.

MINISTERIAL RESPONSIBILITY

IF there is truth in the view that the Restoration largely restored the power of parliament, it might be said in the same vein of paradox that the Revolution was as much a confirmation of the monarchy as an assertion of the power of parliament. William was in principle as free as any of his predecessors to choose his own ministers. Nevertheless, the fact that he owed his throne to parliament, and the continual necessity he was under to come to parliament for supplies and for a renewal of his powers of military discipline, inevitably tended to increase his dependence on parliament.

At first, William chose his ministers so as to obtain the largest amount of support in and out of parliament, rather than for their administrative ability. The resulting ministries – if we may use the term merely collectively to indicate his ministers – consisted of men of all points of view, Whigs and Tories. At the same time, William insisted on keeping foreign policy in his own hands. But the Commons, armed with their re-discovered power to control supply, were by no means willing to acquiesce in their exclusion from foreign policy and launched furious attacks on the ministry. Consequently William found himself obliged to seek means of obtaining the support of parliament, and the changes he made in his ministry in 1694 show that he was aware of the fact. The new ministry was not by any means homogeneous, but at least it was more acceptable to parliament. Nevertheless, disharmony arose again, and the pressure of opposition to his policy in parliament obliged him to take further steps to gain its support. The last of the Tories were dismissed from office, and a ministry was appointed which could rely on the support of the Whig majority in the Commons. Unluckily for William, the elections in the next year resulted in a Tory majority. Although the ministry had no thought of resigning in these circumstances, as a modern ministry would have done, William was obliged to introduce a proportion of Tories to bring it more into line with House of Commons feeling. The refusal of the ministry to resign indicates how little understood was the modern theory of responsibility, but William's partial reconstruction, if we may so term it, at any rate indicates the necessity of choosing ministers agreeable to parliament.

William's half-hearted attempt to obtain parliamentary support for his ministers naturally did little to allay opposition. The problem of ministerial responsibility to parliament remained unsolved, and, in the bitter struggle which ensued, parliament itself sought to provide a solution. To the parliament of 1700 it seemed that the only way to secure responsibility was to insist that all great matters of state should be done in the Privy Council and that 'all resolutions taken thereupon should be signed by such of the Privy Council as shall advise and consent to the same'. It was a harking back over four centuries to the early baronial attempts directly to control the action of the executive. In any case, the attempt to put executive responsibility into the hands of the Privy Council was an anachronism – it was already becoming an increasingly formal body and the real decisions were taken by a smaller group of ministers. The attempt was bound to fail, for it implied that parliament should have the right to call for signed advices, and no minister would accept office on such terms. Had this provision of the Act of Settlement remained in force – it was repealed in 1706 – it would have been fatal to the development of ministerial responsibility.

Equally fatal to the growth of ministerial responsibility would have been another provision of the Act of Settlement, which made holders of places of profit under the Crown incapable of sitting in the House of Commons. It was designed to restrain the undue influence exercised by ministers over the House of Commons through patronage. Had this provision not been severely modified by the Act of 1706, it would have placed the ministry outside parliament and made impossible that close contact between the executive and the legislature, which is the characteristic virtue of the English type of parliamentary government.

By the repeal of these provisions of the Act of Settlement two obstacles in the way of the development of ministerial responsibility were removed. The question whether ministers should be responsible to both Houses or to one remained to be settled. So long as the Whigs predominated in both Houses no clear answer to this question was likely to be given. Queen Anne began her reign with a Tory ministry, but its luke-warm attitude to the war policy obliged her gradually to substitute Whig for Tory ministers. By 1708 the ministry was completely Whig. The general election of 1710 sent up a Tory majority to the Commons. Although the Whig ministers did not at once resign, Anne was obliged by the logic of the situation to form a Tory ministry. The difficulty remained, however, that the House of Lords was strongly Whig, and a struggle between the Houses was inevitable. The issue was brought to the test in 1712, when the Lords threatened to reject the peace of Utrecht. The deadlock was broken by the creation of twelve Tory peers, sufficient to turn the minority into a majority. Henceforward, there could be no doubt to which House in the last resort the ministry would be responsible.

If William and Anne showed an increasing dependence on the support of parliament, yet it cannot be said that their choice of ministers was controlled by parliament. All we can say is that in choosing ministers they had to have regard to the feelings of the Houses and, by the end of the period, more certainly to those of the House of Commons. The way had been prepared for the development of ministerial responsibility, a process which gathered pace

after the accession of George I and was substantially complete by the accession of Victoria.

The Cabinet. The withdrawal of George I from an active
part in government did not in itself alter the constitutional
position. Like his predecessors he chose his ministers and
supported them with all the influence at his disposal. But
his absence from the meetings of his advisers could not but
alter the balance of power. There had been cabinets of a
kind at least since the reign of Charles II, who was wont to
consult a committee of the Privy Council on most, but by no
means all, important affairs. In the reign of William III, as
the importance of the Privy Council declined, that of the
cabinet tended to increase, but its constitutional position
remained unchanged. It was still quite unofficial.[1] Under
Anne the composition of the cabinet came to be more or
less known – it included the heads of government departments and some holders of lesser offices – and it met regularly every week. At the beginning of his reign, George I
appointed a cabinet of fifteen and at first himself attended,
but after 1717 his appearances were rare. The result was to
transform what had been a mere inner group of royal
advisers into a board of government with an independent
existence of its own. Having lost its natural president, it was
inevitable that it should find one of its own, a 'prime
minister' in fact, upon whom would fall the task of co-
ordinating policy, which before had been the king's.

Walpole – 'Prime Minister.' Some modern historians are
inclined to minimize the significance of Walpole as the first
'prime minister'. It is pointed out that the term was
originally one of abuse, applied to Walpole by his enemies
who wished to imply that he was engrossing the chief power

1. Even to-day, when the cabinet has a publicly named membership
and a secretariat of its own, it is still technically unofficial.

in the state. The comparison was with the prime ministers of contemporary France, where the premiership had been established by decree as a definite office to which the other ministers were responsible. But there was nothing official about Walpole's position. Nevertheless there was justification for imputing to him the powers of a prime minister.

Walpole's pre-eminence originated in 1721, when he was appointed First Lord of the Treasury in a new ministry, because he was the only man capable of dealing with the financial situation after the South Sea Bubble. He proceeded to procure the dismissal of his more eminent colleagues until, in 1730, he was without a rival. In the Commons his leadership was unchallenged, and his influence with the king was paramount. It was with some justification that in 1741 Samuel Sandys, in an Address to the king to remove Walpole, could declare 'that one person has grasped in his own hands every branch of government; that one person has attained the sole direction of affairs'. But Walpole was not a dictator. His domination over his colleagues was simply a recognition of the fact that ministerial government cannot be carried on without a single directing voice. Though he did not choose his colleagues like a modern prime minister and was dependent on the king for his majority in the Commons, there is this much foundation in the claim that he was the first prime minister.

It was not only his position in relation to his colleagues which was original. His position in the House of Commons was something new. Before his time the principal ministers had always been in the House of Lords, and if, at the moment of their appointment, they were members of the Commons, it had been the invariable rule to raise them to the peerage soon afterwards. The experience of William and Anne in forming ministries had shown that this arrangement was not without its difficulties, for it left the policies of the government to be defended in the Commons by the less important and influential members of the ministry. The innovation in the case of Walpole consisted precisely in the fact that, when he was appointed First Lord of the Treasury in 1721, he was not raised to the peerage. He deliberately remained in the Commons in order that he might manage them in the royal interest. He was in fact, as he was also called, 'Minister with the King in the House of Commons'.

The choice of Walpole to manage the Commons was dictated by his parliamentary ability. The choice of the office of First Lord of the Treasury as the post in which he should exercise this function was due not to the administrative importance of that post, but mainly to the fact that this minister disposed of the largest amount of patronage. Walpole is sometimes described as the first to organize the distribution of places and, though it may be fairer to say that he inherited the system from his predecessor, the Earl of Sunderland, he certainly devoted a great deal of attention to this matter. For the distribution of royal patronage to members and their clients filled the place which is taken in modern politics by the party machine. It is possible to be shocked by this system (as indeed it is possible to be shocked by the modern system), but the important thing for the historian is that in default of parties bound together by more or less clearly defined political principle, the patronage system made ministerial government workable. Before Walpole there had been constant friction between the House and the government. The effect of his system was not to corrupt the members in the sense that he was able to buy their consciences – most of them were too rich and too independent to be so treated – but it did enable him to maintain some kind of loyalty and coherence among his supporters.

Walpole's position as chief defender of the government in

the House of Commons reacted in turn upon his position in relation to his colleagues. It was soon found to be inevitable that he should assume a responsibility for ministerial policy far wider than that implicit in his Headship of the Treasury. Thus, when George I and Lord Townshend negotiated an alliance with France in 1725 and a great storm of criticism arose, it naturally fell to Walpole to defend the treaty in the Commons, although he had taken no part in the negotiations or indeed in foreign policy at all before this time. In the words of Hervey 'though Lord Townshend only was the transactor of these peace and war negotiations, yet the labouring oar in their consequences always fell on Sir Robert; it was he who was forced to stand the attacks of parliamentary inquiry into the procedure of making these treaties; it was he who was to provide the means necessary to support them; on him only fell the censure of entering into them, and on him lay all the difficulty of getting out of them'.

Walpole succeeded in managing the Commons for an unbroken period of twenty-one years. The manner of his fall is no less illustrative of the new conceptions which were taking shape. In 1739 a violent opposition to Walpole's peace policy arose within and without parliament. Twice Walpole offered his resignation to the king, twice it was refused, and war with Spain was begun against his better judgment. Nevertheless, Walpole could still maintain a majority in the Commons and he still enjoyed the confidence of the king. For three years he hung on in face of increasing opposition. On January 28, 1742, he was defeated by a majority of one, and on February 2 by a majority of sixteen. Walpole then resigned. A modern prime minister would have resigned three years earlier, and so far Walpole's behaviour, though in advance of contemporary theory, lagged behind modern practice. But his eventual resignation demonstrated, in rudimentary form no doubt, the fundamental principle of ministerial responsibility. In the last resort the policy of the government rested on the support of the Commons.

At first there was an attempt in the Commons to revive the ancient weapon of impeachment, but it was perfectly clear that Walpole had committed no crime against the state and what was at issue was the policy of a ministry. The critics had to be content with an inquiry into his conduct during the last ten years – and only a small majority could be found to carry this motion. The committee, hampered by its lack of power to compel evidence, produced only a mildly damaging report, and there the matter dropped. The new method of enforcing ministerial responsibility had been affirmed once and for all. No attempt was ever afterwards made to revive impeachment for this purpose. It had been discovered that the proper way to enforce ministerial responsibility is to compel a minister to resign. It should, however, be noted that only Walpole, as the chief of the king's ministers, was compelled to resign, and his resignation was followed not by anything like a complete change of ministry but only by a certain re-shuffling of posts. At this period there was no notion that his colleagues ought to resign with him. The conception of collective ministerial responsibility only developed slowly. In the whole of the eighteenth century there are only two instances of a complete change of ministry – at the accession of George I, in 1714, and in 1782.[1]

The Whig Supremacy – Political Stagnation: 1742–60. The position established by Walpole was based on his outstanding ability in managing the Commons. Quite clearly, the nature of that position must depend largely on the personal quali-

1. Most but not all of the leading ministers resigned in 1746, when the king refused to confer office on the elder Pitt.

ties of its holder. For some time after Walpole, none of the leaders of the ministry could equal his personal ability, and for that reason some of the progress towards the modern conception of prime ministership was lost. But the essentials remained. For the greater part of the rest of the century there was a leader of the ministry who could be called prime minister, and he nearly always occupied the office of First Lord of the Treasury. Doubtless, some were stronger leaders than others, but we can say of most that they were preeminent and had a certain voice in the choice of their colleagues. However much men might consider the name 'prime minister' discreditable, the reality and the expediency of the thing gradually came to be recognized. Forty years later, when Lord North was attacked for being 'prime minister', though he denied the charge, yet he was constrained to admit that the alternative, 'government by departments', that is, by ministers severally and not collectively responsible to the king, was not altogether satisfactory. Lord Chancellor Thurlow was probably the last minister to assert his independence of his colleagues. For persistently voting in the Lords against bills which Pitt had supported in the Commons, he was finally dismissed in 1792. By the end of the century it had become clear that the solidarity of the ministry was based on the leadership of the prime minister. In 1803 Pitt spoke of 'the absolute necessity there is in the conduct of the affairs of this country that there should be an avowed and real Minister, possessing the chief weight in council and the principal place in the confidence of the King. And that minister ought', he added, 'to be the person at the head of the finance'. Since the beginning of the nineteenth century, the prime minister has usually been associated with the office of First Lord of the Treasury.

The principle that the support of the House of Commons is necessary for a ministry, first recognized in Walpole's time, was steadily maintained. In 1746, when George II refused to confer office on the older Pitt, Pelham and his principal colleagues resigned. The king tried to form a new ministry, but when it failed to receive the support of the House of Commons, he was compelled to recall the old ministry. A similar incident in 1757 proves the same point. When in that year the king tried to get rid of Pitt, and dismissed him from office, he was obliged to take him back, because of his popularity in the Commons and because he was the only minister capable of carrying on the government in the Commons.

Final Victory of the Commons: 1760–1832. The years following the accession of George III in 1760 used to be regarded as a period of reaction from the point of view of constitutional advance. It is certainly true that George III appointed ministers of his own choosing, whose business it then became to find support in the Commons. In the words of Burke, 'The power of the Crown, almost dead and rotten as Prerogative, has grown up anew with far more strength and far less odium under the name of influence'. The selection of the Earl of Bute to be Pitt's colleague in the Secretaryship, the resignation of Pitt and the promotion of Bute to the First Lordship of the Treasury represent the attempt to restore freedom of choice in the appointment of ministers. In Lord North (1770) George III found another prime minister of the same type who would faithfully perform the functions of a 'chief responsible agent of the king's business in parliament' or a 'benign bailiff of royal power'. He had some qualifications to manage the Commons and was a good debater. In 1778 North became convinced that the continuance of the war in America 'must end in ruin to His Majesty and the country' and, like Walpole in similar circumstances, did not feel called upon to resign merely on that account. But in 1782, as a result of a series of disasters abroad, opposition to the ministry gained strength. A motion to end the war was carried in the Commons and another declaring the House's lack of confidence in the ministry was barely defeated. In these circumstances, North and almost all of his colleagues felt obliged to resign. It was a remarkable precedent. North himself stated in the House and told the king that ministers must have the confidence of parliament. It was the first time that the Commons had been virtually able to force the entire ministry to resign merely because they disliked its policy.

The sequel was an even more impressive demonstration of the decline in the power of the king to choose his ministers. It was also an indication of a growing corporate sense on the part of ministers. The king gave the vacant offices to the leader of the Opposition and he was able to retain only one of the old ministers, the Lord Chancellor. Moreover, Lord Rockingham, the new First Lord of the Treasury was able, as the condition of accepting office, to impose conditions and to force on the king a detailed pro-gramme of foreign and domestic policy. A year later the Commons had another opportunity of showing their strength. They were able effectively to register their disap-proval of the ministry's peace negotiations by compelling the king to dismiss it and to choose another which contained not one of the old ministers.

The triumph of the Commons, however, was by no means final. The rejection of Fox's India Bill by the Lords in 1783 gave the king the opportunity to dismiss his ministers once more, and to appoint the younger Pitt his prime minister. The Commons were furious. Resolution after resolution was passed declaring that the continuance of the new ministry in office was 'contrary to constitutional principles and injurious to the interests of His Majesty and his people', and insisting that the ministry must have the confidence of the people, though the king's final right to choose his ministers was never challenged. The king remained firm, refused to dismiss ministers against whom the Commons could bring no charge, and dissolved parliament. The ensuing election gave a large majority in favour of Pitt, who remained at the head of the administration until 1801. Once more the ability of the government to influence the elections had been proved, though on this occasion Pitt's popularity outside the House had counted for much. The Commons, however, continued to press their claim to determine the complexion of the ministry. In 1807, when George III replaced the ministry of All the Talents by a Tory ministry under the Duke of Portland, the Commons protested their 'deepest regret', and Sir Samuel Romilly asserted that 'it was of the greatest importance to His Majesty that the doctrine of responsible advisers should be strictly maintained'. From the occasion in 1829, when George IV, after a prolonged struggle, finally gave his consent to the bill for the Emanicipation of Roman Catholics, we may say that the power of the king to control the policy of his ministers ceased. After the passing of the Reform Bill, which finally destroyed all possibility of influencing elections in the royal favour, the power of the Commons to determine the complexion of the ministry was placed beyond a doubt.

Although the claim of the king to choose his ministers was thus finally disposed of, and the dependence of the ministry on the House of Commons was broadly recognized, the closeness of this dependence was not immediately perceived. In 1841 Lord Melbourne's ministry suffered several defeats in the House of Commons without resigning. In the debate on the motion of lack of confidence which Peel then moved, Macaulay argued that 'the first duty of the minister of the Crown is to administer the existing law' and that a government is not 'bound to resign because it cannot carry legislative changes'. But this was almost the last occasion when such a line of argument could be urged. Since 1841 it has been the rule that the defeat of the ministry on an important legislative measure necessitates its resignation. Such apparent exceptions as there have been are to be explained by special circumstances.

CHAPTER VII

THE COMMONS REPRESENT
THE PEOPLE

To the Knights, Citizens and Burgesses in Parliament assembled ...

Thus, Gentlemen, you have your duty laid before you, which it is hoped you will think of; but if you continue to neglect it, you may expect to be treated according to the resentments of an injured nation; for Englishmen are no more to be slaves to Parliaments than to Kings.

Our name is Legion. And we are Many.

Attributed to DEFOE

Is the House of Commons to be re-constructed on the principle of a representation of interests, or of a delegation of men? If on the former, we may, perhaps, see our way; if on the latter, you can never in reason stop short of universal suffrage; and in that case, I am sure that women have as good a right to vote as men.

S. T. COLERIDGE

IN the previous chapter we have tried to give an account of the way in which the ministry came to be responsible to the House of Commons. We have now to describe the manner in which the House of Commons came to be responsible to the nation. The Reform Act set in motion the process whereby the composition of the House gradually came more or less accurately to reflect the nation at large. At the same time a technique was found for ensuring that the policy of the government was endorsed by a majority of the nation. In this chapter we shall give some indication of the way in which the House of Commons could be responsive to public opinion before the Reform Act, and trace the early history of parties. Then we shall describe briefly the electoral reforms of the nineteenth century. Finally, we shall show how the electorate was enabled to secure that the government is composed of men whose general policy it has approved, and what part was played by the party system in achieving this result.

EARLY HISTORY OF REPRESENTATION

REPRESENTATION is implicit in the earliest form of parliament. In the period before the Commons arrived, the whole nation was conceived to be present in the king's great councils and to assist in their deliberations. When the Commons arrive there is no doubt that the representative principle is present. The main purpose of summoning the Commons was to gain their assent on behalf of the counties and towns to the granting of an aid. The relationship between electors and elected was clearly brought out in 1339, when the Commons declared themselves unable to make the grant demanded without consulting their constituencies and asked for another parliament to be called so that they could do so. The appearance of the common petition in 1327 and the legislative activity of the Commons in the fourteenth and the first half of the fifteenth century are evidence of the responsiveness of members to the interests of the electorate.

The payment of members by their constituencies helped to effect a certain bond between them. 'Wages', said Prynne, 'begat a greater confidence, correspondence, and dependence between knights, citizens and burgesses, than when or where no wages or expenses were demanded and received, as due by law; and gave the electors who paid just occasion to check them or detain their wages in case of absence, neglect, or unnecessary protraction of their sessions'. We have referred in an earlier chapter to the practice in the fifteenth and early sixteenth centuries of members making a report on the business of the parliament on their return home. The representatives of the City of Lincoln who returned from the parliament of 1523 told their fellow citizens what they 'have done in the parliament, and that there is now owing to them for their expenses twelve pounds'. The relation between the members' account of their work and their expenses is plain. But soon after this time wages ceased to be paid, and that desirable dependence of members upon their constituents to which Prynne refers was no doubt weakened.

In matters of local, as opposed to national, interest there was at all times a close tie between the member and his constituency. The vast mass of petitions from cities, towns, groups and individuals in the first two centuries after the arrival of the Commons is sufficient testimony of this. In 1572 the House resolved to sit from three to six o'clock in the afternoon to proceed only with private bills, and it was ordered that the House should not 'go to the question of any such bill, if it concerned a town or shire, unless the knights of such shire or shires, or the burgesses of such town or towns be then present'. In the same spirit, two centuries later, in 1793, an order of the House excused members from attendance on election committees, if they were engaged on the urgent business of their constituents in committees on private or local bills. The vast output of local acts in the eighteenth century is proof, if proof were necessary, that in matters of local concern the tie between members and their constituents was as great then as at any time.

Though there was never a time when the counties and boroughs could not influence members in national questions, it is to the period after the Restoration, when parties were beginning to form, that we must look for the origins of the closer and more continuous modern relationship. The letters of Andrew Marvell to the citizens of Hull are the classic evidence. At the beginning of the session of 1669 he writes to the mayor to ask that, 'if there be any particular that may more nearly relate to your affairs, you will be

pleased to consider thereof briefly, so that I may be instru-
mental to serve you therein as far as my capacity will carry
and my obligation binds me'; and, at the beginning of the
next session, he similarly places himself at the disposal of
his constituents. On these occasions he clearly referred to
matters of local interest, but later in the session of 1670 he
sought their views upon a wider kind of issue: 'What is your
opinion at home of the bill from the Lords for general
naturalization of all foreigners that shall take the oath of
allegiance and supremacy? We [sc. the Commons] have not
yet given it a hearing.' The inquiry reflects the feeling in
the country at this time against foreigners and papists.
Eight years later the same feeling, raised to fever pitch by
the allegations of Titus Oates, burst out in the agitation
for the Exclusion Bill. At the elections in 1678–79 'candidates came under engagements to gratify the wishes of the
people, by a diligent investigation of the plot and a zealous
prosecution of its authors',[1] and at the elections of 1681 'in
many places it was given as an instruction to the Members
to stick to the bill of exclusion'.[2]

But the emergence of local interest in national politics at
this time was, like the appearance of parties, historically
premature. After the Revolution there were no great
political questions to divide the country into true parties,
and, correspondingly, instances of public opinion being
brought to bear upon political questions are few. In 1701,
when it was still possible to be anxious for the permanence
of the Revolution settlement, the City of Westminster
instructed its members that 'they endeavour to support His
Majesty's title, and defend the nation against the French
King'. This was hardly a positive programme, but still it
was an expression of political feeling; and there were
similar instructions to members from Buckinghamshire and

1. Somerville, *Transactions*, 78.
2. Burnet, *History of His Own Time*, II, 127.

Cornwall. The impeachment of Dr Sacheverell by a Whig House of Commons in 1710 for his sermons inculcating the doctrine of unlimited passive obedience was undoubtedly responsible for the return of a Tory majority at the ensuing election. In 1713 the electors of the City of London asked their members to make a rigorous inquiry into the late Tory ministry and into the responsibility for advising the Peace of Utrecht. The Excise Bill of 1733 was the occasion of a general outburst of instructions to members. 'Most of the boroughs in England and the City of London itself', wrote Lord Hervey, 'sent formal instructions by way of memorials to their representatives, absolutely to oppose new excises and all extensions of excise laws.' This agitation was successful: the nearness of a general election doubtless helped to reinforce it. After Walpole's resignation in 1742 there was a widespread demand for a regular programme of reform. More than forty constituencies urged their members to make a strict inquiry into the late administration, to restore triennial parliaments, and to pass the pension and place bill which Walpole had resisted. Popular clamour procured the repeal of the act for the naturalization of the Jews in 1755. On this occasion Lord Hardwicke commented: 'However much the people may be misled, yet in a free country I do not think an unpopular Measure ought to be obstinately persisted in.' The popular will could on occasion make itself effective even in a period when the House of Commons was notoriously unrepresentative.

How little responsive to public opinion the House could be is shown by George II's remark to the elder Pitt during the Seven Years War (1756–63): 'You have taught me to look for the sense of my subjects in another place than the House of Commons.' Indeed there was a definite trend of feeling among members against the propriety of constituencies giving instructions to them. It is clear from statements of the time that members were reluctant to admit anything like a close or continuous control over their actions in the House. Sir William Yonge, in a speech in opposition to annual parliaments, in 1745, stated the view that 'after a gentleman is chosen, he is the representative, or, if you please, the attorney of the people of England, and as such is at full freedom to act as he thinks best for the people of England in general. He may receive, he may ask, he may even follow, the advice of his particular constituents; but he is not obliged, nor ought he to follow their advice, if he thinks it inconsistent with the general interests of his country.' Yonge was perhaps more concerned to emphasize the priority of national over local interest. Thirty years later, in his famous speech to the freemen of Bristol, Burke stated the doctrine of free responsibility, if we may so style it, with greater emphasis: 'Authoritative instructions, mandates issued, which the member is bound blindly and implicitly to obey, to vote and to argue for, though contrary to the clearest conviction of his judgment, and conscience – these are things utterly unknown to the laws of the land, and which arise from a fundamental mistake of the whole order and tenor of our Constitution.'

Burke's became the generally accepted view of the Whig party, but, though largely through his influence the practice of instructing members was dropped in the last quarter of the eighteenth century, there was undoubtedly a steady growth in the power of public opinion. The case of Wilkes showed the power which popular feeling could exert. Three times Wilkes was elected in the years 1768–9, and three times the House refused to let him sit, but the House was eventually constrained to admit him, and a few years later a resolution was carried not merely vindicating Wilkes, but declaring that the proceedings against him were subversive of the rights of the whole body of the electors of the kingdom. It was a triumph of democratic principle, but it was short-lived. The intensive efforts of George III to control the

government by influencing elections and the reaction inspired by the French Revolution combined to nullify the
power of popular feeling. It was only after 1815 that the cry
of 'Economy and Reform' was heard again, and the agitation revived which culminated in the Reform Act.

REFORM OF THE ELECTORAL SYSTEM

In the fourteenth and fifteenth centuries the shire representation remained unaltered. Thirty-seven counties returned
two knights apiece. By the enfranchisement of Wales, Mon-
mouthshire, and Cheshire Henry VIII brought the number
of county members up to 90.

The borough representation was less clearly defined. The
writ to the sheriff merely ordered him to return two knights
for the county and two burgesses for each borough, with the
result that, in the absence of an authoritative list of
boroughs, there was a considerable degree of uncertainty
and variation in the boroughs returning burgesses to parliament.

The first complete (except for London) list of towns returning members is for 1295, and this indicates that 116
towns returned 234 members. But, as we have suggested,
the 'Model' was no model for future parliaments: from
1327 to 1437 the number of boroughs making returns is
fairly constant at about 95, and the number of members
at about 190. From the middle of the fifteenth century the
numbers steadily rose until by 1530 they had reached the
'Model' level: 117 boroughs returning 236 members. From
the middle third of the fifteenth century onwards it is clear
the towns are beginning to value parliamentary representation. Plymouth, which had not been represented since 1313,
and Windsor not since 1340, had begun to return members
again by 1442. Coventry, which had been without representation for a hundred years, reappeared in parliament in

1453. The charter which New Woodstock obtained in the same year was perhaps the last to include a clause exempting a town from the duty of sending burgesses, and in the 1460s representation in parliament was a right which began to be sought and granted in charters.

The sixteenth century saw a remarkable increase in the borough representation. Besides creating 13 Welsh boroughs Henry VIII also gave representation to a number of English towns: Berwick, Buckingham, Chester, Lancaster, Newport (Cornwall), Orford, Preston and Thetford. So keen was the demand of the gentry for seats in parliament that the Crown was tempted to enfranchise quite insignificant townships. Thus of the 17 boroughs created by Edward VI, 7 were in sparsely populated Cornwall; and of Mary's 14 new boroughs 4 were in Catholic Yorkshire. The largest addition was made by Elizabeth I, of whose 31 new boroughs 6 were in Cornwall. By the end of her reign the total number of borough members had risen to 374, making with the 90 county members a House of Commons of 464.

That the borough representation was too high was already recognized in the reign of Queen Elizabeth. When the Earl of Rutland asked for parliamentary representation for Newark, Wylson, one of her secretaries of state, in refusing the request wrote: 'it is thought that there are over many [i.e. burgesses] already, and there will be device hereafter to lessen the number for the decayed towns'. No 'device', however, was made. James I appears to have been equally conscious of the need for reform. When he summoned his first parliament, in 1604, he ordered the sheriffs not to send 'a writ to any ancient town, being so ruined that there were not residents sufficient', and refused to assent to a bill to enfranchise the County Palatine of Durham on the ground that the House of Commons was already too large, and that there were places like Old

Sarum which ought to be disfranchised. Cromwell's attempt to correct the abuses of the electoral system was overthrown at the Restoration. Reform was urged at the Revolution of 1688, at the Union with Scotland in 1707, and again in 1800 at the Union with Ireland. But in all this period, right down to the Reform Act of 1832, apart from the throwing of a few corrupt boroughs [1] into the counties, the system of representation in England remained unchanged. If the anomalies of the system were already patent in the time of Elizabeth it may easily be imagined how glaring they had become in the course of two and a half centuries of social and industrial change. The more picturesque examples are well known: Old Sarum, whose fields could not even provide a shelter for the returning officer, Gatton with its half-dozen electors. On the other hand, large and increasing towns like Manchester, Leeds, Sheffield and Birmingham were without separate representation. The Society of the Friends of the People estimated that in 1793, 51 English and Welsh boroughs, comprising less than 1,500 voters in total, sent 100 representatives to Westminster.

More serious still than the merely numerical anomalies of the representative system were the abuses to which it gave rise. The smaller the electorate in any constituency the more open it was to influence. The counties, which possessed a fairly wide franchise, based upon the possession of freehold land worth 40s. a year, were free from the most serious forms of corruption. Though perhaps the majority of county seats were held by the great landowners, yet they could be retained only by a certain regard for the interests of the electors. Even a hereditary seat could not be retained without effort and expenditure. In any case there was a considerable convergence of opinion between the elector and the elected arising from their common agricultural interest. It is significant that throughout the whole of the reform

1. New Shoreham in 1771, Cricklade in 1782, Aylesbury in 1804.

period the counties were never once attacked. They were regarded as providing the healthiest element in parliament because, though they might be subject to influence, they could not be simply bought.

The boroughs, on the other hand, possessed widely differing franchises and were correspondingly subject to varying degrees of influence. Only a small minority, the open boroughs, as they were called, where the franchise was extremely wide, in some cases amounting to manhood suffrage, could claim even a relative independence. At the other end of the scale were a small number of burgage boroughs where the right to return a member approximated most nearly to the private property of a family or an individual. In between these two classes lay a larger class of corporation and freemen boroughs where the franchise belonged to a small body which could be more or less easily controlled.

In the sixteenth century the controlled or nomination boroughs were increasingly sought after by ambitious country gentlemen for whom a seat could not be found in the shires. And since the law which required the representative of a town to be a resident burgess had long been a dead letter, the gentry rapidly obtained a monopoly of borough seats. By the end of Elizabeth's reign four out of every five members were gentlemen; if the law had been observed four out of every five would have been townsmen. The importance of this development for the history of parliament can hardly be overestimated. It goes far to explain the aggressiveness of the lower House in the seventeenth century; and it also made a political career possible for many distinguished parliamentarians, who might not otherwise have found a seat.

Various unsuccessful attempts to reform the system were made from 1762 onwards. The earliest took the form of proposals for punishing bribery, and a few like the act of 1762 actually reached the statute book. The Grenville Act of 1770 provided for the appointment of committees to investigate elections and resulted in the disfranchisement of a few of the worst boroughs. But none of these efforts was really effective. The habit of corruption was too deeply ingrained to be changed by merely penal methods. More radical solutions were needed.

The earliest of these attempts, that of Lord Chatham in 1770, shows clearly where the evil lay. Declaring that the boroughs were 'the rotten part of the constitution', he proposed to counterbalance them by adding a third county member. In 1776 Wilkes proposed a re-allocation of seats more in accordance with the distribution of population. In 1780 the Duke of Richmond produced a scheme which, in addition to a complete redistribution of seats on the lines of equal districts, proposed universal suffrage. In 1782 Pitt moved for an inquiry into the system of representation and made several attempts to introduce a measure of reform, including a bill, all of which were defeated. The French Revolution and the outbreak of war with France in 1793 gave a setback to the movement, and parliamentary action was discontinued. But agitation continued outside parliament, and when the war ended a fresh series of schemes was introduced. None was successful. At last, in 1830, a Whig government was returned to power pledged to correct the defects in the electoral system which had destroyed the 'confidence on the part of the people'.

The preamble of the Reform Act of 1832 indicates four purposes: to redistribute seats in accordance with the changes in population, to increase the number of knights of the shire, to extend the franchise, and to diminish the expense of elections. In fulfilment of these purposes 56 nomination or rotten boroughs with less than 2,000 inhabitants, and returning 111 members in all, were abolished; 30 boroughs with less than 4,000 inhabitants were each deprived of one member; and Weymouth and Melcombe Regis gave up two members. The 143 seats so obtained were distributed as follows: 65 to the counties, 44 to 22 large towns, 21 to 21 smaller towns, 13 to Ireland and Scotland. The borough franchise was made uniform, the right to vote being given to all householders paying a yearly rent of £10. In the counties the vote was given to three new classes: copyholders of £10 annual value, holders of leases of a certain length and value, and annual tenants paying at least £50. The effect of these changes was to increase the electorate by one half, to about two-thirds of a million.

The effects of the Act in removing abuses were not so complete as its friends had hoped or as its enemies had feared. Nevertheless, though the Act had not by any means entirely eliminated abuses, it had made a revolutionary change in the electorate. The counties remained substantially unaltered, but the effect of admitting the £10 occupier to a vote in the boroughs was to enfranchise the middle and lower middle, though not the artisan, classes, of whom indeed a certain number – the ancient right voters – were actually disfranchised.

Though the revolutionary character of the Reform Act in its effects on the electorate is plain, its effect on the character of the House of Commons is less obvious. For the reformed House was drawn from the same classes as it had been before – the country gentlemen and the aristocracy. There was no substantial increase in the number of those drawn from finance, business and manufacture. No doubt this fact had an important bearing on subsequent political development. But the important and essential fact was not that the new House looked like the old, but that it represented a new and growing spirit in the country, which had not hitherto found parliamentary expression. Out of 658 members 500 belonged to the party which had carried the reform. Admittedly the party was far from homogeneous, ranging from Whigs of the old aristocratic type to extreme Radicals on the other flank. Such a combination would be difficult to range on the same side in any other issue. Nevertheless it was 'reform' which had carried the day and the victory in the parliamentary sphere would inevitably open the way to reforms in every other sphere of government, in church matters and in the penal law, in administration and finance, and to further reforms of the electoral system itself. Above all, quite apart from anything that the Reform Act had brought to pass, the circumstances in which it passed demonstrated the triumph of a new element in parliamentary government – the power of public opinion to assert itself.

Though the Reform Act of 1832 did not make any revolutionary change in the character of the House of Commons, and though to the more radical element the results of the Act were disappointing, yet to the vast majority of the House it seemed that a sufficiently large measure of reform had been taken to last for a long time. Indeed to many of those who had supported the reform it must have been something of a relief to discover that its effects were not so revolutionary after all. Consequently the movement for further reform took time, twenty years in fact, to develop, and when it did finally come, it was more as a result of party manoeuvre than of any overwhelming demand for it in the country. Four schemes, three Liberal and one Conservative, all failed between 1852 and 1860, and in 1866 another Liberal bill (Mr Gladstone's) was ruined by the defection of a section of his own party. The Reform Act of 1867 was sponsored by the Conservative Government of Derby and Disraeli. In the counties the leasehold and copyhold qualifications were reduced to £5 a year, and a new qualification was introduced based on the occupation of premises of £12 rateable value. In the boroughs the vote was given to all householders paying rates, whether directly

NOTES ON THE PICTURES

Plate 1. This is the earliest picture of parliament which has much historical value. The original drawing was made by order of Sir Thomas
Wriothesley, who was Garter King of Arms from 1505 to 1534. Standing
behind the traverse on the left of the throne is Tunstall, Bishop of London, who delivered the speech opening the parliament. In front of the
throne on the cloth of state three earls bear the cap of maintenance, the
sword and the Earl Marshal's baton. On the woolsack nearest the throne,
where the Chancellor usually sat, are the two chief justices; and on the
other three woolsacks are the judges and other lawyers. The two kneeling
figures are the Clerk of the Parliaments and the Clerk of the Crown. At
the bottom of the picture the Commons stand at the bar with their
Speaker, Sir Thomas More, at their head (*see* p. 35). This parliament
was opened at Blackfrairs but later moved to Westminster.

Plate 2. This engraving represents the House of Commons which met on
April 13th, 1640, in the Short Parliament. The scene is St Stephen's
Chapel. The heads of two statues have been broken off and the wall-
paintings appear to have been obliterated. The Clerks at the Table are
Henry Elsyng, Clerk of the House, and John Rushworth, who is tradi-
tionally the first Clerk Assistant (*see* pp. 57 and 59). In the foreground,
the Serjeant at Arms, bearing the mace, appears to be escorting a
member who stands uncovered at the bar.

Plate 3. J. Pine's engraving of Gravelot's drawing. It shows how St
Stephen's Chapel looked with the galleries and panelling which are
attributed to Wren.

Plate 4 is also from an engraving by Pine. It shows the White Chamber,
where the Lords sat from the fourteenth century until 1800. On the walls
hang the famous tapestries depicting the Armada, and on the left is the
fireplace which, it is said, was Charles II's favourite place when attending debates.

A. *Cardinal Woolsey.*
B. *Warrham Archbishop of Canterbury.*
C. *Bishops.*
D. *Abbots.*
E. *Barons.*

F. *Prior of S.t John of Jerusalem.*
G. *Earls.*
H. *Duke of Norfolk.*
I. *Duke of Suffolk.*
K. *Garter.*

Plate 1. The Opening of Parliament in 1523.

Plate 2. The House of Commons
in the reign of Charles I.

Plate 3. The House of Commons in 1741/2.

Plate 4. The House of Lords in 1755. The King sitting on the Throne, the Commons attending him at the end of the Session.

Plate 5. The House of Lords in 1808.

Plate 6. The House of Commons in 1808.

Plate 7. The Reformed House of Commons, 1834.

Plate 8. The House of Commons, 7th May, 1940.
(After the painting by John Worsley.)

NOTES ON THE PICTURES – *continued*

Plates 5 and 6 are from *The Microcosm of London*, published by Ackermann in 1808. Pugin the elder drew the architecture, Rowlandson the figures. From 1800 to 1834, the *Lords* sat in the Court of Requests, which stood where the statue of Richard Coeur de Lion now stands. The *Commons* were still in St Stephen's Chapel.

Plate 7. An engraving by William Heath. The following extract from the Journal of February 5th, 1834, explains the incident. 'And words of heat having passed during the debate between Mr *Sheil* and Lord Viscount *Althorp* [Chancellor of the Exchequer], and the honourable Members having been called upon by Mr Speaker to assure the House that they would not prosecute the matter without the Walls of the House, and Mr *Sheil* having declined to give any such assurance, and Lord Viscount *Althorp* not having given a satisfactory assurance to that effect, *Ordered, nemine contradicente,* That *Richard Lalor Sheil,* Esquire, and Lord Viscount *Althorp* be taken into the custody of the Serjeant at Arms attending the House.' The Speaker is Manners-Sutton (*see* pp. 126-7).

Plate 8 is from a painting by John Worsley. The scene is during the debate on the conduct of the war which resulted in Mr Chamberlain's resignation and Mr Churchill's acceptance of the premiership. Mr Churchill can be seen just above the head of the mace. Next him on the left is Sir John Simon and next him again on the left is Mr Chamberlain. The white-haired figure on the Opposition front bench is Mr Lloyd George. Mr Attlee is immediately below the Speaker. Mr Amery is making his peroration in the words which Cromwell used to the Long Parliament: 'You have sat too long here for any good you have been doing. Depart, I say, and let us have done with you. In the name of God, go.' A year later, on May 10th, 1941, this chamber was burnt down in an air raid.

or indirectly as part of the rent, and to lodgers paying £10 a year in rent. The effect of these changes was greatly to increase the number of urban voters in proportion to the rural without increasing their representation. In fact the Act created more anomalies than it removed. In the same year fifty-four borough seats were re-distributed, but it was another seventeen years before a truly systematic scheme of reform was undertaken. This was embodied in two Acts. The Franchise Act of 1884 extended the householder franchise to the counties and brought the number of voters up to five million, or one in seven of the population. By the Act of 1885 a radical redistribution of seats was made on the basis of population. Boroughs of less than 15,000 inhabitants were absorbed in the counties, and larger boroughs received one member for every 50,000 inhabitants. The counties were divided into one-member constituencies. The result of the scheme was to create an electoral system based more or less accurately on population and a nearly uniform franchise.

The final stages by which the present electoral system was reached may be recorded briefly. The system established in 1884–5 continued unchanged for a third of a century. The Representation of the People Act of 1918 abolished the property qualification for members and extended the franchise to women of thirty years of age. In 1928 the age qualification for women was reduced to twenty-one years as for men. The Representation of the People Act, 1948, provided for a re-distribution of seats in accordance with changes in the population, for the abolition of the university constituencies, and for the abolition of the business premises franchise, making residence the sole qualification.

Thus the various anomalies of the electoral system and the abuses to which they gave rise have been eliminated, and it might seem that on the mechanical side, at any rate, there is little room for improvement. It should, however, perhaps be pointed out that the existing system results in a House of Commons which does not necessarily nor in fact accurately reflect the strength of parties in the country. Thus in 1922 the Conservative Party with 38 per cent of the votes returned 56 per cent of the members, and in 1929 the Labour Party with 2 per cent fewer votes than the Conservatives returned 4 per cent more members. Since the war the system has generally worked so as to bring to power the party which won the most votes. Only in 1951 when the votes cast for the two major parties were nearly equal did the one with slightly fewer votes secure more seats. The Liberal Party, on the other hand, has been consistently under-represented. In 1959, for example, the votes cast for Liberal candidates would on a mathematically just system have returned 37 members; in fact only six were elected.

One other electoral reform of the nineteenth century was of the highest importance. Secret voting had been proposed from time to time since Grote urged it in the 1830s. But opposition had always been strong against it on the ground that 'the motives under which men act in secret are as a general rule inferior to those under which they act in public'. In 1852 Palmerston was of the opinion that 'to go sneaking to the ballot box is unworthy of the character of straightforward and honest Englishmen'. At last in 1872 this much needed reform was carried and put an end to the various methods of intimidation which had continued unabated after the Reform Act.

THE PARTY SYSTEM

AT the beginning of this chapter we showed that there was never a period when the House of Commons was not capable of reflecting at any rate strongly-felt popular feeling. And the reforms of the representative system which we have just described produced at any rate a rough correspondence between the electorate and the House of Commons. We have now to give an account of the machinery whereby opinion is organized and translated into actual policies of government – in other words the party system.

Party, in the bare sense of a group of men of similar views and who act together in parliament for common purposes, appears at least as early as the reign of Elizabeth. The Puritans in her later parliaments consistently opposed her prerogative in matters of Church and State. 'It was to this sect', said Hume, 'whose principles appear so frivolous, and habits so ridiculous, that the English owe the whole freedom of their constitution.' This may be putting it too high, but at least the Puritans must be given the credit for initiating the principle on which government by party rests. As an organized party they sought admission to the House of Commons, obtained a majority there and successfully resisted the queen's policies. James I's assertion of divine right and the excesses of the High Church men whom he supported served to develop and broaden the formation of parties. Sandys, Coke, Eliot, Selden and Pym were the leaders of the parliamentary party against the supporters of the Crown. The process was carried further by the arbitrary measures of Charles and the bigotry of Laud, and ended by dividing the whole country between Cavalier and Roundhead.

If it is possible to attribute to the Puritans the distinction of having formed the first parliamentary party, it is in the period after the Restoration that the origins of the two great parties of the eighteenth and nineteenth centuries are to be found. After the fall of the Cabal Ministry in 1673, the Earl of Danby became the king's principal adviser and through him the king, by the use of patronage, tried to maintain a group of supporters in the Commons. At the same time the Earl of Shaftesbury became leader of the 'country' party opposed to the court party. He may thus be regarded as the first leader of a regular Opposition, though we must be careful not to import modern connotations into the term, and contemporary enemies could denounce his conduct as treasonable. It was to the contest of these two parties over the Exclusion Bill of 1681 that the names Whig and Tory owe their origin. The enemies of the Duke of York called his supporters, many of whom were Catholics, Tories, a term hitherto applied to a set of lawless Irish bog-trotters. The Whigs received their name from some supposed comparison with the Scottish Covenanters, called Whiggamores or Whigs, who made an inroad on Edinburgh in 1648.

From their origin in this period the names Tory and Whig acquired the broad connotation which they were to preserve more or less distinctly for 150 years, until they were abandoned for Conservative and Liberal. The essential characteristic of the Tories was their support of the royal prerogative, that of the Whigs the limitation of royal authority. A secondary distinction was religious: the Tories leaning towards High Church principles, the Whigs looking more favourably on the Protestant forms of Dissent.

But though the names served to indicate these broad distinctions of outlook, they did not by any means indicate two clearly cut parties. The high-handed action of James II served to unite the parties in a common resistance to royal pretentions, and the Revolution was the work of a coalition. The Revolution, by removing the fear of autocratic government, largely removed the basis of their difference. The Tories, following their tradition, naturally supported the Crown. The Whigs, jealous though they would be of kingly rule, could not afford to attack the guardian of the glorious constitution. And the religious differences were beginning to lose their force. Thus the effect of the Revolution was to throw the parties into confusion, and far from members of the two Houses being clearly divided into two camps, they fell into innumerable changing groups: 'Whig, Tory, Old Ministry, New Ministry, Hot Whigs, High Fliers, October Club, Moderate Men, Old Whigs, Modern Whigs, and such like' – as one writer described the situation of parties in 1712; or, on the religious basis of classification given by a contemporary observer in 1702: 'Churchmen, High Churchmen, Low Church, Non-Conformists, Cavaliers and Sneakers'.

William III owed the throne to a coalition and not unnaturally preferred mixed ministries, which he succeeded in obtaining during most of his reign, though the disadvantages of such a policy were apparent after 1700. Anne indeed preferred the Tories but wished not to be too dependent on them. 'Her plan was not to suffer the Tory interest to grow too strong, but to keep such a number of Whigs still in office as should be a constant check upon her ministers.' [1]

If the circumstances of the first two reigns after the Revolution were not such as to encourage the development of parties, the total discredit of the Tory Party for its suspected Jacobitism after 1715 retarded the process for another fifty years. The great Chatham was averse to all party connexion, and it was his follower Lord Shelburne who uttered the famous dictum: 'Measures not men.' By the middle of the century the repute of party had reached its lowest point. In 1751 Horace Walpole wrote: 'all was faction, and splitting into little parties ... Opposition ... and even the distinction of parties having in a manner ceased at this period!' And, when Newcastle proposed the organization of an opposition in 1757, Hardwicke professed himself shocked at the suggestion.

George III, in his attempt to restore royal control of

1. Sheridan, *Life of Swift*, pp. 124–5.

government, naturally exploited this state of affairs, and in appointing Chatham to office in 1766 told him that he relied on him giving 'his aid towards destroying all party distinctions'. It was only the crisis of 1770 that compelled Chatham to modify his aversion to party. Burke was the first to acknowledge its necessity and to recognize its use. Dismissing Shelburne's dictum as venerable cant, he affirmed that 'party divisions, whether on the whole operating for good or evil, are things inseparable from free government'. While recognizing the dangers of 'the narrow, bigoted' spirit to which party is liable, he clearly distinguished it from faction. In his famous definition, 'Party is a body of men united, for promoting, by their just endeavours, the national interest, upon some particular principle in which they are all agreed'.

The Mandate. The mere development of parties with more or less definite points of view was not in itself sufficient to effect the expression of the popular will in the government of the country. In order for this to be achieved it was necessary that another principle should come to be recognized, the principle that elections are fought not merely on the basis of personalities, nor even of parties, but of parties expressly committed to definite policies. This is the principle of 'the mandate'.

The passing of the Reform Act itself marked a step in the direction of the mandatory principle. Only three years before (in 1829) Wellington and Peel had carried the Catholic Emancipation Act in direct violation of their promise at the previous election. When he introduced the Reform Bill in 1831 Lord Grey considered himself 'pledged to it when out of office, and still more when in office, from a sense of public duty', even though it had not expressly been placed before the public as an issue at the election of 1830. At the election of 1831 reform was definitely made the issue.

In the king's speech dissolving parliament it was expressly stated that the issue was not this or that ministry but whether the Reform Bill should be passed. Indeed it was the complaint of the Duke of Wellington that the question was not even the general question of reform – for that had been decided by a majority in the previous House of Commons – but whether a particular scheme of reform embodied in a bill should be passed. The placing of an issue in such detail before the electorate, unconstitutional as it might seem to some, was certainly unprecedented.

The principle thus introduced, namely that the votes given at an election could determine a question of policy, was not fully appreciated at once. Cobbett was one of the few who did. 'If the House of Commons had not been pledged', he wrote in *The Political Register* of that same session, 'we should have no Reform Bill ... everything depends upon the manner in which the new body of electors are disposed to exercise the power which is now placed in their hands of choosing proper persons to represent the wants, interests and opinions of the whole community in the reformed House of Commons.'

It was not to be long, however, before the occasion arose which would show clearly the importance of the new principle. In 1834 Peel found himself unexpectedly appointed Prime Minister at a time when parliament was not sitting. Perceiving that he could not maintain a majority in the House, and being unable to explain his programme in parliament, he and his colleagues decided to issue a declaration of policy in the form of a manifesto to his constituents at Tamworth. This manifesto created in the words of Greville 'a prodigious sensation'. A writer in *The Quarterly Review* wrote: 'When before did a Prime Minister think it expedient to announce to the people, not only his acceptance of office, but the principles and even the details of the measures which he intended to produce? ... The new cir-

cumstances in which the Reform Bill has placed the Crown,
by making its choice of Ministers immediately and absolutely dependent on the choice of the several constituencies,
and, in the first instance, quite independent of the concurrence of the assembled Parliament, have rendered such a
course not merely expedient, but inevitable.'

In spite of this clear exemplification of the new principle
its practical consequence, namely the inevitability of a dissolution when a ministry ceases to command a majority in
the House of Commons, was not immediately recognized.
Thus, in 1841, when Peel moved a motion of want of confidence in the Melbourne administration, he stated that he
did not consider that if the motion were successful it would
be a proper occasion for a dissolution. Sir John Hobhouse,
on the other hand, speaking for the ministry, urged the
contrary proposition and pointed out the inconsistency of
Peel's present view with the principle implied in the Tamworth manifesto of 1834. In the event the more modern
view prevailed and in the queen's speech dissolving parliament it was said, in very general terms, to be sure, that an
election was to be held in order to ascertain 'the sense of
my people upon matters which so deeply concern their
welfare'.

Again, in 1846, when he brought in his proposal for
abolishing the Corn Laws, Peel refused to have an election
on this issue, although at the last election he had expressed
himself as opposed to any such measure. 'I thought such an
appeal', he wrote afterwards, 'would ensure a bitter conflict
between different classes of society, and would preclude the
possibility of a dispassionate consideration by Parliament,
the members of which would have probably committed
themselves by explicit declarations and pledges'. So retrograde a view at this stage of parliamentary history seems
astonishing to the modern reader. Peel still clung to the old
view, already obsolete, that a dissolution should not be

advised unless there were a reasonable chance of success for the ministry, because 'unsuccessful dissolutions are, generally speaking, injurious to the authority of the Crown'. His chief loyalty, he felt, was to the Crown, not to the people.

Indeed, the modern view that a general election is necessary to validate new policies did not gain complete acceptance till 1886. In that year Mr Gladstone introduced his Home Rule Bill, to which no reference had been made at the election of 1885, and attempted to defend his action by analogy with the introduction of the first Reform Bill. When, however, the bill was defeated on second reading Gladstone did not hesitate to advise dissolution. Significantly he called it 'the people's dissolution'. In the following election campaign he stated unequivocally that the issue before the electorate was the establishment of a legislative body in Ireland for the management of exclusively Irish affairs. Since this time the right of the people to have all major questions of legislative policy put before them at an election has never been challenged.

Party Organization. Though the effective operation of the party system cannot be said to have begun until the period of Disraeli and Gladstone, the organization of parties had steadily developed since the Reform Act.

Of party organization in the eighteenth century we may fairly say there was none. The ministerial party regularly met before the opening of the session to hear and also to discuss a statement of policy, and the Opposition held similar meetings. A certain amount of election campaigning in the country was also undertaken from the time of Walpole. It is only after the Reform Act that party organization begins to appear. In 1834 the Conservatives raised a central election fund, and in 1835 they formed local organizations. But it is to Disraeli that party organization in the modern manner is due. In 1852 he employed Philip Rose, a solicitor, to reorganize the party in the country, and in 1867 the National Union of Conservative and Constitutional Associations was established. The Conservative Central Office was set up after the defeat of the Conservatives in 1868. The Liberals were somewhat later in the field of organization. In 1861 they instituted a Registration Association, and in 1877 Joseph Chamberlain founded the National Liberal Federation.

The foundation of the National Liberal Federation marks a new phase in the development of party organization. Hitherto candidates had offered themselves for election without adoption by a local body. From 1880 onwards it became the practice for local associations to adopt candidates and to require them to conform to the party programme. This has become a permanent feature of the modern party system. But the Federation also undertook to exert its influence on the formation of party policy, and in the period 1883–95 was considerably successful in inflicting the views of the associations on the party leaders. The inconvenience of such pressure to the organizers of the party and the weakness of hotch-potch policies formed in this way led to the curtailment of the influence of the local associations, and the formation of policy was placed in the hands of the central body, the Organization Committee.

The intensive methods invented by Chamberlain were followed by the Conservative Party. As in the Liberal Party, it was found necessary to take steps to repress the influence of the associations and the Central Office occupies a position similar in regard to policy to that of the Organization Committee of the Liberals. The Labour Party differs in important points of organization from both the other parties, and as a consequence of its respect for the decisions of the majority its discipline is stricter than that of the older parties. The election manifesto to which candidates are required to subscribe is decided by the National Executive

Committee on the basis of resolutions passed at the annual conference.

Her Majesty's Opposition. 'Party' has thus become an essential element of parliamentary government. But when we speak of 'the party system' as practised in this country we mean something more than the mere existence of parties. A multiplicity of parties makes good government impossible and, though the periods of only two parties have been short, the efficiency of the system depends on the prevalence of two major alignments. There must be a government side sufficiently united to carry out a common policy, there must be an opposition strong enough to make effective criticism. There is a sense indeed in which the existence of an organized opposition may be regarded as the essential characteristic of the British system of parliamentary government. Without it parliament cannot perform its proper function of criticism, and to be responsible criticism must be that of a body of men able to form an alternative government. Hence the extraordinary status accorded to the opposition in parliaments formed on the British model. The expression 'Her Majesty's Opposition', first coined by Sir John Hobhouse in 1826, has become the official title of the government's chief critics, and the payment since 1937 of a salary out of public funds to their leader marks him out as at least a potential prime minister.

CHAPTER VIII

THE INDEPENDENCE OF
THE SPEAKER

I loved independency and pursued it. I kept firm to my original Whig principles, upon conscience, and never deviated from them to serve any party cause whatsoever.   ARTHUR ONSLOW

THE outstanding qualities of the Speakership in modern times are its independence and impartiality. These requisites are so well understood and so uniformly available that we are apt to take them for granted. But the Speaker has not always been the independent arbiter we know, and the process by which he has become such was long.

EARLY HISTORY OF THE SPEAKERSHIP

IN an earlier chapter we noted the election of one of their number to report their answers to the king as evidence that the Commons had begun to develop a corporate activity. Some such 'prolocutor' must have been chosen from the earliest times, but it was in the Good Parliament of 1376, when the Commons sat for the unusual length of ten weeks, that the Speaker emerged as something more than a mere occasional mouthpiece. In that parliament Sir Peter de la Mare led the Commons in a bold attack upon the government. He was not, like a modern Speaker, elected at the beginning of the parliament. Each time he came before the Lords he spoke of himself as having been appointed 'for this time' or for 'to-day', yet his outstanding position as leader of the Commons justifies us in calling him the first Speaker, though the records do not give him that name. His successor in the parliament of 1377 is the first to be described as holding any such position: '*Monsieur Thomas de Hungerford, chivaler, qui avait les paroles pour les Communes.*'

Fortunately we know enough about de la Mare and Hungerford to be able to form an idea of what the Speakership meant in this its earliest phase. De la Mare was the steward of the estates of the Earl of March, and it is clear that when he attacked the government he did so less as a champion in the cause of national grievances than as the agent of a baronial faction, the faction which served the interest of the Prince of Wales. For when the Prince died and his party fell to pieces, de la Mare's fortunes sank with it – he was arrested and imprisoned in Nottingham castle. In the succeeding parliament the opposite party was in the ascendant, and Hungerford, as steward of its leader, the Duke of Lancaster, was elected Speaker of the Commons. The first two Speakers were in fact the managers of the Commons on behalf of their masters in the Lords.

Just as it was a baronial rebel who had first brought the Commons to parliament and showed to kings the value of enlisting their support, so it was the baronial politicians of a century later who taught the Crown the way to manage them. During Richard II's minority the Speakers seem to have been non-political administrators, but in his later parliaments, when he began to assert his personal rule, we find Sir John Bussy, one of his devoted servants, is Speaker.

The precedent set by Richard became a tradition under the Lancastrian kings. The Speakers in their parliaments were regularly men who had had employment in the royal service. It is clear, moreover, that the fifteenth-century Speaker is no mere official, he is an active politician subject to all the hazards of politics. Bussy, William Tresham, Thomas Tresham, Thorpe, Wenlock and Catesby all came to violent ends on the scaffold, in civil war or by assassination.

In the Tudor period royal influence in the choice of the Speaker becomes abundantly plain. Sir Thomas Lovell had been on the winning side at Bosworth and was afterwards made Chancellor of the Exchequer for life. Empson and Dudley, the notorious servants of Henry VII, were elected Speaker in spite of their unpopularity. Thomas More was already sub-Treasurer to the king when he was elected Speaker in 1523; for his services in the matter of the subsidy he received £100 more than the usual fee, and a year later he was made Chancellor of the Duchy of Lancaster. In the Reformation Parliament the Commons chose Thomas Audley whom, the king said, he knew, 'since he was in his service, to be both wise and discreet'. Sir Richard Rich, Speaker in the parliament of 1536, was duly rewarded for his sycophancy with the Chancellorship. In fine, the Tudor Speaker was first and last a royal servant, paid for his services and afterwards rewarded with great office. In the time of Edward VI the £100 which he received for the session is described as his 'accustomed fee and reward'. In the reign of Elizabeth he is actually named in the House by one of the royal officers, though the form of an election is still retained. Lambarde, who was a member in 1562–3 and 1566, explains how this was contrived: a member of the Privy Council reminded the House of the royal command freely to choose a Speaker but 'commendeth in his opinion some person by name'. Once indeed, in 1566, objection was taken to the election of the nominee (Onslow) on the ground that he was a serjeant-at-law and therefore owed his duty to the Lords, but without success; and in 1597 when the Comptroller of the Household rose to propose Mr Serjeant Yelverton, the Commons 'hawked and spat', but proceeded to elect him unanimously. Coke, writing about 1628, described the established practice as a mere formality similar to the *congé d'élire* of a bishop.

THE ELIMINATION OF ROYAL INFLUENCE

As the contest between king and Commons developed in the reigns of the first two Stuarts, the position of the Speaker as the servant of the Commons on the one hand, and of the king on the other became increasingly difficult. The crisis came in Charles' third parliament. For a while Charles was able to prevent the Commons from bringing their discontents to the point of a decision by ordering Speaker Finch to adjourn the House. But a second attempt to thwart the Commons by the same method was resisted. Finch was forcibly held in the chair while another member put the question. 'I will not say I will not,' Finch exclaimed, 'but that I dare not.'

Cromwell continued the tradition of governmental influence and Lenthall was chosen Speaker on his recommendation. It was not in fact until the third parliament of Charles II that the first step was taken towards the removal of royal influence. Sir Edmund Seymour, who had been Speaker in the second parliament, was again proposed in 1678–9 as 'being a person acceptable to the king' and was elected by the Commons without demur. When, however, the Commons presented him in the House of Lords, the Chancellor declared him to be unacceptable to the king, and on their return to St Stephen's, they were informed that His Majesty recommended Sir Thomas Meres. The Commons protested. 'It is the understood right of the Commons', they said, 'to have the free election of one of their members to be their Speaker, to perform the service of the House ... The Speaker so elected, and presented according to custom, hath by the constant practice of all former ages, been continued Speaker and executed that employment, unless such persons have been excused for some corporal disease, which has been allowed by themselves, or some others on their behalf in full parliament.' Declaring that 'all this is but loss of time', the king brusquely rejected the protest and prorogued parliament for several days. When parliament reassembled, the Chancellor once more directed the Commons to choose a Speaker, and again the royal recommendation was announced in their House. This time a new candidate was named, Mr Sergeant Gregory, and was unanimously elected. Both sides had made some concessions, but the Commons had maintained their claim.

Though in the contest over Seymour the Commons had been successful in asserting their right, it was long before royal influence was eliminated from the election of Speakers. Court influence was exerted in the elections of Speakers in 1701 and 1705; in the Parliament of 1722–7 Walpole told Onslow, who was ambitious to be Speaker, that 'the road to that station lay through the gates of St James's'; and in 1780 George III, consistently with his policy of controlling parliament by every available means, fair or corrupt, used influence to secure the election of Cornewall. Nevertheless, 1679 marks the end of the practice of openly announcing the royal preference in the Commons. When in 1694 the Comptroller of the Household attempted to impose the royal nominee upon the House, the Commons promptly protested against the practice and elected a member of their own free choosing – Foley.

THE SPEAKER GIVES UP POLITICAL ACTIVITY AND PARTY CONNEXION

IN the second phase in the development of the Speakership, it gradually came to be seen that the Speaker ought to abstain from political activity and connexion with party. While the Speaker is in the chair and acting as the president of a deliberative assembly, impartiality is obviously the essence of his function. What we have to study is not so much the behaviour of the Speaker in the chair, but how this requirement of impartiality during debate necessitated his abandonment of political activity when not in the chair. This was a long and slow development, by no means a continuous forward movement, and progress depended largely on the personal character of the individual Speaker. The ground gained in the advance towards independence made by a Speaker of outstanding personality was not necessarily held by the next. Our account will consist of a record of those Speakers who contributed most to the formation of the rule of abstention from politics.

Hooker, describing the office of Speaker in the reign of Elizabeth for the benefit of the Irish House of Commons, said that 'during the time of the Parliament he ought to sequester himself from dealing or intermeddling in any public or private affairs, and dedicate and bind himself wholly to serve his office and function'. But this was a counsel of perfection, far in advance of anything which Hooker can have experienced in England or could have expected in Ireland.

Foley. It is significant that the beginning of independence can be dated from the Speakership of that Paul Foley upon whose acceptance by the Crown the Commons successfully insisted in 1694. He indeed was so independent that it was counted his greatest fault that he paraded this quality too ostentatiously. Nevertheless, he did not feel called upon to forgo his rights as a private member in committees of the whole House. Foley's immediate successors contributed little towards raising the Speaker's office above politics, and intervention in debates in committees of the whole House continued to be normal. It is to the Speakership of Arthur Onslow that we must look for the next great advance.

Arthur Onslow (1728–61). Hitherto it had been by no means unusual for a Speaker to hold office at the pleasure of the Crown. And so when Arthur Onslow accepted the office of Treasurer of the Navy a few years after his first election to the speakership, he did nothing irregular. But in 1742, stung, it is said, by the taunt that he had used his casting vote under the influence of the Crown, he resigned the Treasurership. Whether or not we accept this explanation of his motive in resigning, it is certainly true that no Speaker after Onslow held an office at the pleasure of the Crown, though other offices under the Crown might be held long after his time. It was still possible in the early years of the nineteenth century for Speaker Abbot to hold a lucrative sinecure in the Irish establishment during his tenure of office.

The story of Onslow's resignation is in keeping with all that we know of his behaviour as Speaker. Throughout his thirty-three years' tenure of the Speakership he exhibited an unflinching attitude of independence towards the government, and he enforced the rules of procedure without respect of persons. 'The forms of proceedings', he held, 'as instituted by our ancestors, operated as a check and control on the action of ministers, and they were in many instances a shelter and a protection to the minority against the attempts of power'. Only by strict adherence to the rules of procedure could the minority be protected from those 'irregularities and abuses which these forms are intended to check, and which the wantonness of power is but too often apt to suggest to large and successful majorities'. Indeed, so great was Onslow's attachment to forms that Horace Walpole said that 'it often made him troublesome in matters of higher moment'. There could hardly be better testimony to Onslow's indifference to ministerial convenience.

Another innovation of Onslow's, though not of itself important, serves to illustrate his original and independent temper. It had long been the custom at his election for the Speaker to make a formal protest of unworthiness. In the course of time this courteous form had come to be triplicated: the first plea of unworthiness was made when he was proposed for election, the second after election in a speech from the step of the chair, and the third after taking the chair, when he sought the House's permission to intercede with His Majesty to command the Commons to proceed to another election. In 1728 and 1735 Onslow followed the custom and made the prescribed three excuses, but at his election in 1741 he omitted the third and contented himself with an expression of thanks to the Commons. Onslow's precedent was not invariably followed by his immediate successors, but Addington (1789–1801) was the last to revert to the former usage.

The House was not unappreciative of Onslow's efforts to elevate the office of Speaker. When he retired in 1761 he was voted a pension of £3,000 and the precedent has been followed in favour of every subsequent Speaker.

Payment of Salary to Speaker. The giving of a pension on retirement was a step in the direction of making the Speakership a worthy object of ambition in itself, rather than merely a step in the course of a career. But it was not until thirty years later that the independence of the Speaker was fully secured by giving him a generous salary. Up to 1791 the Speaker's remuneration had derived partly from the fees for private bills, which at that time averaged £1,232 a session, partly for various allowances: £5 a sitting day from the Exchequer, £100 per session for stationery, and £1,000 at the beginning of a new parliament for equipment. Each Speaker also received a service of plate estimated in 1790 as worth £1,000; and two hogsheads of claret, and a buck and a doe from the royal forests annually. For these miscellaneous emoluments the Act of 1790 substituted a fixed salary of £6,000.[1] At the same time the self-denying precedent set by Onslow was made a legal obligation;

---

1. Reduced to £5,000 in 1834.

a clause in the Act forbade the Speaker to hold any place of profit under the Crown during pleasure.

Thus the formal guarantees of the independence of the Speaker were established, but it was to be many years before the modern standard of conduct was attained. Nothing can detract from the greatness of Onslow's achievement in raising the level of independence, but it is only fair to point out that his Speakership coincided with a period of low political temperature. In the whole of his career as Speaker there were only two occasions when genuine political feeling, as opposed to mere party intrigue, seriously disturbed the House: Walpole's Excise Bill of 1733, and the bill for the naturalization of Jews in 1753. We must not be surprised, therefore, if the standard he set was not immediately established. Cust, his immediate successor, was a nonentity; Fletcher Norton's unrelenting hostility to George III earned his defeat when he sought re-election in 1780; Charles Wolfron Cornewall had the voice and presence required of a Speaker, but these advantages were offset by his habit of drinking porter while in the chair; Addington was active in committee and incompetent in the chair.

Abbot. With the turn of the century the trend towards independence was resumed. Not that Charles Abbot (1802–17) was a Speaker of the type of Onslow, determined to demonstrate his impartiality at all costs. He was not. But by this time the feeling of the House, and of the world outside the House, was beginning to demand something of the standard of conduct required of a modern Speaker. Abbot was much interested in measures for purifying the House of Commons, and it is in the light of this interest that his extraordinary behaviour in connexion with Grattan's bill of 1813 for Catholic Relief is to be judged. At the committee stage of the bill he made a powerful speech against the clause enabling Catholics to sit and vote in either House of Parliament, and this speech undoubtedly contributed in large measure to its rejection. In this intervention in committee there was nothing irregular at this period. What was unexpected and shocked contemporaries was his reference in terms of evident satisfaction to the defeat of this bill in his address to the Prince Regent at the end of the session. In the debate on a motion disapproving of his conduct, Abbot urged that in the past Speakers had regularly given a general account of all the principal proceedings of the Commons during the session, but he was unable to produce a single instance of the Speaker making a partisan speech on such an occasion. The motion was defeated by 274 votes to 106, and Abbot escaped formal censure. But the voting hardly indicated the true feeling of the House in the matter. As one contemporary wrote: 'The great majority in favour of the Speaker seems to denote either that the House in general regarded him as blameless, or that the weight of his character, and the connexion of his honour and reputation with those of the body over which he presided, rendered, in the opinion of the greater number, a public censure inexpedient or indecorous. Yet upon perusing the speeches made on the occasion, few, it is imagined, will be insensible of a great superiority in point of argument as well as of eloquence on the side of reproof: and were the question referred to the public at large, it can scarcely be doubted that the decision would be that the Speaker had been betrayed by party zeal – for his honourable character will not admit a more unfavourable interpretation – into a step at least improper and of dangerous example, if not unconstitutional. The discussion of the subject will have a good effect if it prevent the recurrence of anything similar.'

Manners-Sutton. Charles Manners-Sutton (1817–34), was the last Speaker of the old type. In the chair his reputation

for impartiality was unchallenged. Out of the chair he saw
no reason to refrain from the keenest partisanship. He
intervened in committee on three occasions, but it is significant that on each the issue was religious, and he felt it
necessary to make some apology. Nor did he withdraw
from the counsels of his party, which twice offered him a
place in the administration.

Shaw-Lefevre – the first modern Speaker. To Shaw-Lefevre,
1839–57, is due the initiation of the last phase in establishing the Speaker's independence of party. That the Speaker
should refrain from political action in the House had already
before his time become the accepted practice. Shaw-
Lefevre completed the process by insisting on severing
all connexion with party in or out of the chair. To him is
due the modern conception which requires the Speaker to
abstain from any kind of political activity.

It is the corollary of this conception that a Speaker should
not have to fight an election. Since 1832 this has been the
general rule, but there have been exceptions, as in 1885
(Peel), 1895 (Gully), 1935 (FitzRoy), 1945 and 1950
(Clifton Brown), 1955 (Morrison).

AUTHORITIES FOR CHAPTERS VI—VIII

EMDEN, C. S. *The People and the Constitution,* 1956.

HALÉVY, E. *History of the English People in 1815,* 1924.

KEIR, D. L. *Constitutional History of Modern Britain Since 1485,*
1960.

MAY, T. ERSKINE. *Constitutional History of England,* 1912.

NAMIER, L. B. *The Structure of Politics at the Accession of
George III,* 1929.

NEALE, J. E. *The Elizabethan House of Commons,* 1949.

PORRITT, E. *The Unreformed House of Commons,* 1903.

THOMSON, M. A. *Constitutional History of England, Vol. IV,
1642–1801,* 1938.

CHAPTER IX

THE MODERNIZATION
OF PROCEDURE

To be a slave of old traditions is as great a folly as to be a slave of new quackeries.   STUBBS

THE broad outlines of bill procedure and the rules of debate, as we saw in Chapter IV, had already been established by the time the Commons transferred themselves to St Stephen's, and in the course of the seventeenth century considerable progress was made in the organization of the House for the conduct of business and in the development of financial procedure. Though a full study of the subject has yet to be made, it is probably true to say that the corpus of rule and practice thus established continued with little alteration until the nineteenth century.

PROCEDURAL REFORM, 1800–77

Arrangement of Business. In the seventeenth century and earlier the arrangement of business was in the hands of the Speaker, though the House might on occasion make general orders for this purpose or for giving precedence to certain bills. The House sometimes set up a business committee, as for example in 1571, to arrange the order in which bills were to be considered, or, as in 1621, 'to consider of the State of all the Business of the House and ... to report, which Businesses they think fittest to have Priority'. It was the practice to give precedence to public bills over private.

In the eighteenth century the House began to take a greater interest in the arrangement of business and the

Speaker's part in it correspondingly declined. A distinction was drawn between 'Order Days' and 'Notice Days'. On Order Days only that business could be taken which had been set down by order of the House. On Notice Days new business could be taken. In the course of the century it became the practice to reserve two days a week – Mondays and Fridays – for ordered business. Since it was within the power of the majority to determine the orders to be taken the general effect was to give precedence to Government business on Order Days. Even this modest recognition of the Government's claim to have time set apart for its necessary business did not pass without criticism. In 1811, when the usual motion was made that on Mondays and Fridays precedence should be given to business set down by order of the House, Mr Whitbread complained that 'the portion of the week claimed by the Minister was much too large, and curtailed greatly the space allotted for the discussion of all the multifarious relations of national policy. ... It went to deprive the House of its vitality.' The argument has a modern sound. Similar objections have been urged on every occasion during the last hundred years when the government has asked the House for time.

The first task of the reformed House of Commons was to devise better arrangements for conducting its business. Both parties, the Conservatives, as they were now called, led by Sir Robert Peel, and the Whig-Liberal majority, felt the need of reforms in its time-table, if the House was to perform its work efficiently. Accordingly in the first days of the session Lord Althorp as Leader of the House brought forward a number of proposals, which were adopted with some modifications. It was decided that the House should meet regularly at five o'clock on five days of the week for the public business set down in the order book. Private business and petitions – the latter had become a great burden – were relegated to the afternoon sittings from twelve to three. Committees were given power to sit from ten to five and also during the sittings of the House.

Standing Orders. Before 1832 the procedure of the House of Commons was governed in the main by a few traditional rules which, elaborated and developed by successive interpretations and Speakers' rulings, formed an unwritten code of procedure. In the seventeenth century this unwritten code was supplemented from time to time by orders relating to business or procedure which become part of the code. In the eighteenth century it was felt necessary to define the financial rules of the House and to embody them in Standing Orders, binding from session to session and enforceable *au pied de la lettre*. These are the oldest of the existing Standing Orders relating to public business. After 1832 it was clear that the traditional processes of procedural development by way of precedent and casual improvization were no longer adequate to achieve the radical changes which the pressure of business demanded. The House for the first time in its history set about deliberately creating and reforming its own procedure. Select committees were set up at frequent intervals – there were seven [1] in the fifty years after the Reform Act – to examine one or another aspect of business. Those recommendations of these committees which the House adopted became Standing Orders. By the end of the century the Standing Orders relating to public business had grown to nearly a hundred.

Orders of the Day to be read without Question put. The first of these procedure committees, that of 1837, was appointed 'to consider the best means of conducting the public business with improved regularity and despatch'. The committee found that the two days on which it was customary to allow the government precedence for its business had

1. In 1837, 1848, 1854, 1861, 1869, 1878 and 1886.

been largely invaded by the discussion of other subjects, which it was possible for a member to raise by way of amendment to a question for reading a government order of the day. The committee therefore recommended that such amendments be out of order except on the question for going into Committee of Supply or Ways and Means – exceptions which they felt it was necessary to retain in order to give members an opportunity to raise such matters as they should desire. The House accepted this recommendation. In 1848 an order was made directing the Clerk to read out the orders of the day without any question being put, and this order has been a Standing Order since 1853. The effect of these Orders was to achieve a greater certainty in the arrangement of business.

Elimination of Superfluous Questions. It was soon realized that this limited reform did not provide adequately for the growing volume of business, and in 1848 another committee was appointed. The situation with which the committee was faced is described in the evidence which Speaker Shaw-Lefevre gave before it:

The Business of the House seems to be continually on the increase. The characteristic of the present session has been the number of important subjects under discussion at the same time and adjourned debates on all of them. This intermingling of debates, adjourned one over the head of the other, has led to confusion, deadening the interest in every subject, and prejudicing the quality of the debates on all. Motions to adjourn the House for the purpose of speaking on matters not relevant to the prescribed business of the day are made more often than formerly; and motions to adjourn the debate have become of late years much more frequent.

To remedy this difficulty Shaw-Lefevre suggested that debate should not be allowed on motions for adjournment, and that before resuming debate on any subject a motion might be made 'that this debate shall not be further adjourned'. This would in effect have been a kind of closure and was rejected as too drastic. The Speaker also proposed that the number of questions at the various stages of a bill – there were eighteen questions at this time exclusive of those on amendments – should be drastically reduced. This suggestion was more favourably received, and as a result the question upon the first reading of a bill was made unamendable and undebatable, and the question, 'That the bill be engrossed' was entirely abolished. But perhaps the most important outcome of this committee was the new rule that, when an order was read for the House to resolve itself into committee for the further consideration of a bill, the Speaker was to leave the chair without question put. The significance of this rule, which afterwards became known as the 'rule of progress', was that it eliminated the prevalent abuse of the old-established practice whereby it was possible to re-open the whole question of a bill's merits each time the House went into committee on it.

Thus by the middle of the century considerable progress had been made in the way of modernizing procedure. Nevertheless much remained to be done. Giving evidence before the select committee of 1854 Mr (later Sir) Thomas Erskine May described the situation as follows:

When the greater part of these ancient forms were adopted, the proceedings of the House were very different, in many respects, from what they are at present. Motions were made without notice – there were no printed votes – the bills were not printed – petitions relating to measures of public policy were almost unknown – parliamentary reports and papers were not circulated – strangers were excluded, and debates unpublished. In all these respects the practice has changed so materially that I think a smaller number of forms is now necessary than probably was found consistent with due notice to every one concerned in former times.

May therefore proposed the abolition of all unnecessary forms, especially those questions which lent themselves to obstruction. The committee acted upon this suggestion, and as a result a whole series of unnecessary questions was abolished, including those for reading a bill a first and second time in committee of the whole House, on first reading of new clauses, and on reports from committee of the whole House.

Restriction of Amendments on going into Committee of Supply. The most important of the proposals put forward by May in 1854 was that after the first occasion the question 'That Mr Speaker do now leave the chair' on going into Committee of Supply should be abolished, that is to say, that the 'rule of progress', which had already been applied to going into committee of the whole House on a bill, should be extended to the Committee of Supply. Since 1811, when the setting aside of two Order Days in the week had curtailed the freedom of members to raise subjects on these days, the practice had grown up of raising subjects on amendments to the question that Mr Speaker do leave the chair on going into Committee of Supply, and in this way members endeavoured to recoup themselves for the loss of opportunities on Order Days. The growth of this practice had become a serious impediment to the dispatch of business. In the words of the Speaker: 'The practice has been carried to an inconvenient extent, especially of late, when members have not been contented with merely moving amendments on going into Committee of Supply, but have given previous notice of their intention to call the attention of the House to questions before the Speaker leaves the chair, which has caused very great delay and inconvenience. Many topics may thus be debated by the House at the very same time, without its being able to give an opinion on them. Some of those subjects may refer to the conduct of the government, and require a member of the government to take part in the debate; but as no member of the government can speak more than once upon the same question, and as all these subjects are brought forward upon one question, it frequently happens that the

House is obliged to listen to *ex parte* statements which cannot be answered.' In spite, however, of the strong advocacy of the Speaker and the Clerk, the committee felt unable to accept the proposed reform and the practice went on unchecked.

In 1861 the problem was tackled by another procedure committee, which included among its members Lord Palmerston, Mr Disraeli, Mr John Bright, Lord Stanley and Sir George Cornewall Lewis. Once again May urged the inconvenience of the existing practice. But this committee, despite its distinguished membership, while recognizing the force of May's argument, was unable or unwilling to provide a remedy. 'It must be remembered', they said, 'that the statement and consideration of grievances before supply are among the most ancient and important privileges of the Commons, and this opportunity of obtaining full explanation from the Ministers of the Crown is the surest and the best'.

At length, in 1882, it was provided that the motion 'That Mr Speaker do now leave the Chair' should only be moved on *first* going into Committee of Supply on one of the main branches of the Estimates (i.e. Civil, Navy, Army, and later Air). In recent years, however, it has been felt that the debates on these four occasions could be more conveniently held *in* Committee of Supply on specific Votes. Thus the ancient right of Members to raise grievances before granting supply has virtually disappeared.

OBSTRUCTION AND DISORDERLY CONDUCT, 1877–88

THE procedural developments of the period 1877–88 were directed against the obstructive tactics and disorderly behaviour of the Irish Nationalist Party. Although obstruction on the scale and of the persistency practised by this party was something new, obstruction as a parliamentary weapon of occasional use was not without precedent. In 1641 the debate on the Grand Remonstrance went on from three o'clock in the afternoon till the following morning, by which time, Rushworth tells us, the House looked like a starved jury. In 1771 Edmund Burke boasted that posterity would bless the persistence with which he and a few others divided the House twenty-three times in a debate on the publication of parliamentary proceedings in newspapers, which lasted till five o'clock in the morning. The possibility of using the forms of the House for delaying proceedings was envisaged by the order of 1717: 'that when the House, or a committee of the whole House, shall be sitting, and daylight be shut in, the serjeant at arms attending the House do take care that candles be brought in without any particular order for that purpose'.

In 1806 Castlereagh and others endeavoured to neutralize the influence of the radicals in a Coalition government by night after night making 'long speeches on no particular occasion, inflicting unbearable weariness upon the ministerial ranks, until Sheridan, as a sort of despairing joke, proposed that the burden should be distributed by the process of forming relays of attendants'.[1] In 1831 Sir Charles Wetherall kept the House up till half-past seven in the morning in order to delay the committee stage of the Reform Bill. Obstruction was first used by the Irish in 1833, when they succeeded in protracting the first reading of Earl Grey's Irish Coercion Bill over seven sittings by threatening to make repeated motions for the adjournment of the House, if any attempt was made to curtail discussion. The committee stage and third reading were made to take a whole month by similar tactics. An equally strenuous resistance was made to the Irish Arms Bill of 1843, upon which forty-four divisions were forced during the committee stage by a minority which was never greater than twenty.

1. Harris, *History of the Radical Party in Parliament*, p. 84.

When therefore, in 1877, Parnell and half a dozen of his countrymen decided to embark upon a course of methodical obstruction, they were not entirely without precedent. Beginning with the more innocent kinds of obstruction which consisted simply in moving a large number of amendments to bills with a fair show of relevance and reason, he soon passed to the more mechanical methods. His most successful effort was on July 2 in Committee of Supply, when, by alternately moving 'that the Chairman do now leave the Chair' and 'to report progress', Parnell and his friends managed to spin out the sitting from two in the afternoon till seven in the morning. When reproached with systematic obstruction Parnell frankly declared his 'special satisfaction in preventing and thwarting the intention of the Government'.

Rule against moving two Dilatory Motions on the same Question. Such tactics it was clear were not to be endured, and before the end of the month the House had adopted two new Standing Orders by overwhelming majorities. One was that which forbade a member to move 'That the Chairman do report progress' or 'That the Chairman do leave the Chair' more than once or to move both during the debate on the same question, or to speak more than once to such a motion.

'Naming' a Member for disregarding the authority of the Chair. The other Standing Order adopted at this time provided that if a member after twice being out of order should be pronounced by the Speaker (or the chairman) to be disregarding the authority of the chair, a motion should be put to the House without debate 'that the Member be not heard during the remainder of the debate'. This, however, was not found to be sufficiently stringent and after experience of further obstruction the House adopted the resolution which is the basis of the present Standing Order No. 22. The operative words of this Standing Order which have remained practically unaltered to this day are: 'Whenever

any Member shall have been named by Mr Speaker ... as disregarding the authority of the chair, or abusing the rules of the House by persistently and wilfully obstructing the business of the House, then ... Mr Speaker shall forthwith put the question, on a motion being made, no amendment, adjournment or debate being allowed, "That such Member be suspended from the service of the House".'

These measures, however, were insufficient to break the campaign of obstruction, which was now raised to the highest pitch. The sitting which began at four o'clock on Monday, January 24, 1881, ended at half past nine on the following Wednesday morning, when Speaker Brand interrupted the member who was then in possession of the House and forcibly brought the sitting to a close with these words:

The motion for leave to bring in the Protection of Person and Property (Ireland) Bill has now been under discussion for above five days. The present sitting, having commenced on Monday last at 4 o'clock, has continued until this Wednesday morning, a period of forty-one hours, the House having been frequently occupied with discussions upon repeated dilatory motions for adjournment. However prolonged and tedious these discussions, the motions have been supported by small minorities in opposition to the general sense of the House. A crisis has thus arisen which demands the prompt interposition of the Chair and of the House. The usual rules have proved powerless to ensure orderly and effective debate. An important measure, recommended in Her Majesty's speech nearly a month since, and declared to be urgent in the interests of the state by a decisive majority, is being arrested by the action of an inconsiderable minority, the members of which have resorted to those modes of obstruction which have been recognized by the House as a parliamentary offence. The dignity, the credit, and the authority of this House are seriously threatened, and it is necessary that they should be vindicated. Under the operation of the accustomed rules and methods of procedure the legislative powers of the House are paralysed. A new and exceptional course is imperatively demanded; and I am satisfied that I shall best carry out the will of the House and may rely upon its support if I decline to call upon any more members to speak, and at once proceed to put the question from the Chair. I

feel assured that the House will be prepared to exercise all its powers in giving its effect to these proceedings. Future measures for ensuring orderly debate I must leave to the judgment of the House. But I may add that it will be necessary either for the House itself to assume more effectual control over its debates or to entrust greater authority to the Chair.

Mr Gladstone's Procedural Reforms, 1882. The crisis had been reached. It was clear that piece-meal measures would not suffice, and in 1882 Mr Gladstone brought forward a comprehensive scheme of reform, consisting of twelve resolutions. Six whole sittings during the course of the session were devoted to their discussion but, when the summer recess arrived, nothing had been achieved, and an autumn session had to be arranged specially to deal with procedure. At the end of six weeks' discussion the resolutions were made Standing Orders.

Of these new Standing Orders, three merely extended or strengthened existing rules. Thus the rule made in 1877 against making two dilatory motions on the same question was now extended to all proceedings whether in committee or in the House, and debate on such motions was confined strictly to the matter of the motion (see p. 136). Likewise the Standing Order enabling the Speaker to 'name' a member for disorderly conduct was made more severe (see pp. 136–7); and 'the rule of progress' (see p. 132) was at last applied to going into Committee of Supply.

The revolutionary character of Mr Gladstone's reforms was due to the introduction of three entirely new rules:

(1) *Urgency Adjournment Motions.* The old freedom of members to move the adjournment of the House, which had been found so serious an embarrassment to the dispatch of business, was severely restricted. Such motions could in future be moved only after Questions, and only for the purpose of discussing a matter which in the opinion of the Speaker was definite and of urgent public importance.

(2) *Irrelevance and Tedious Repetition*. The Speaker was empowered to direct a member to discontinue his speech for irrelevance or tedious repetition.

(3) *The Closure*, which has now become a normal instrument for the curtailment of debate, had been suggested as early as 1848 (see p. 131). As brought in by Mr Gladstone it gave the Speaker power on his own initiative to propose the question, 'That the question be now put', that is to say, to bring the debate to a close. If this motion was supported by a majority consisting of not less than 200 members, it was to be carried. The experience of the next five years, however, seemed to show that the application of the rule placed too great a strain on the impartiality of the Chair, which only used it twice in that period. Accordingly, in 1887, Mr W. H. Smith, on behalf of the Conservative government, proposed that the initiative should be given to any member, only the Speaker's concurrence in accepting the motion being necessary. This proposal was strongly opposed and the debate on it occupied fourteen sittings, but it was eventually carried, substantially in the form of the present Standing Order. It was said in the debate, that by this rule the House had 'placed its business entirely in the hands of the Government', since it could always command the requisite number of votes. Nevertheless in the following year the closure was made easier to obtain by reducing the number needed to vote in the majority from 200 to 100 – the present figure.

The Guillotine. The closure even in the more stringent form adopted in 1887 proved inadequate to deal with relevant obstruction of the kind developed by Parnell, and the Salisbury government were driven to seek yet other remedies. After thirty-five sittings spent in the discussion of the Criminal Law Amendment (Ireland) Bill, Mr W. H. Smith moved a motion to the effect that at ten o'clock on June 17,

the chairman should put all questions necessary to complete the committee stage of the bill. The motion was carried, and at the appointed time the discussion was finished, when only six clauses had been debated, and the remaining fourteen were put through in a matter of minutes. This procedure, known usually as the 'guillotine', had only been used once before (in 1881) and to a contemporary historian it seemed 'a desperate expedient for carrying out the inflexible will of the majority'.[1] Though it cannot be regarded as a normal part of parliamentary procedure, the guillotine has been used whenever systematic obstruction threatened to hold up government business unreasonably. In 1947 Standing Orders provided for the appointment of a business committee to settle the details of the time-table laid down by the order of the House, and for applying the guillotine to proceedings in a standing committee.

Hour of Rising Fixed. By 1888 the House had come to the conclusion that a complete scheme of procedural reform, dealing with every aspect of its business and not merely designed to deal with the evils of obstruction, could no longer be delayed. Accordingly priority over all other business was given to the discussion of the rules and a complete scheme of reform was undertaken. This scheme included and substantially re-enacted the various rules against obstruction which had been made in 1882 and introduced a new rule not specifically directed against obstruction but closely related in purpose. The necessity for a regular time for terminating the sitting had long been apparent. It was now made a rule that the Speaker should bring the sitting to a close at 1 a.m. without any question put. The present Standing Order fixes the time for the automatic adjournment of the House at 10.30 p.m.

1. Redlich, *Procedure of the House of Commons*, 1908, vol. I, p. 181.

STANDING COMMITTEES

THE proposal that public bills should be referred to select committees had been suggested to the Procedure Committee of 1848 by the Clerk of the House. 'Whenever', May argued, 'you can avail yourselves of the services of a select committee instead of a committee of the whole House, it is an advantage.' But the proposal seemed too revolutionary and was not adopted. May put it forward again in 1854 and 1861, and was strongly supported by the Speaker on both occasions. Some bills at any rate, it was urged, could suitably be sent to select committees, for example, consolidation bills. It was pointed out that private bills, many of which dealt with important matters of trade and public welfare, had long been dealt with successfully by committees of five. The procedure committee were impressed and made a recommendation in this sense, but in spite of strong support it was rejected by the House. In 1878 May brought forward the idea once more, but in a new form. His original idea had been to refer public bills to small select committees like those used for private bills. He now proposed that committees 'of considerable size should be constituted mainly of members permanently sitting and competent to represent the general opinion of the House, aided by members appointed specially to serve in regard to particular bills'. This was the essence of the standing committee system as it eventually came to be accepted by the House. The idea was not, however, adopted until 1882, when it was embodied in Mr Gladstone's scheme. This scheme, which provided for two standing committees, one for bills of a legal character, the other for bills dealing with trade, was tried in 1883, but fell into abeyance until 1888 when it was re-introduced by Mr W. H. Smith.

Committal to a standing committee did not, however, become the normal procedure for public bills until nearly twenty years later. In 1907 Sir Henry Campbell-Bannerman brought in a comprehensive scheme for developing the use of standing committees along the lines upon which they work at the present day.

Under this system all public bills except the annual financial bills go to a standing committee unless the House otherwise orders. Six or seven standing committees are usually set up each session and are designated by the letters of the alphabet except the Scottish Standing Committee to which are committed bills relating only to Scotland. Originally conceived as committees of which the greater part remained unchanged throughout the session, standing committees have now lost all claim to the title 'standing'. Since 1960 the whole membership of each standing committee has been specially appointed for each bill. Each committee, except the Scottish, consists of not less than twenty nor more than fifty members nominated by the Committee of Selection, who must have regard to their qualifications and the composition of the House. The Scottish Standing Committee consists of not less than thirty members representing Scottish constituencies together with not more than twenty other members, chosen in the same way. The chairmen of standing committees are appointed by the Speaker from a panel and are changed for each bill. The procedure in a standing committee follows that of a committee of the whole House and the chairman has powers similar to those of the Chairman of Ways and Means.

Since standing committees sit in the mornings and can also, if necessary, sit in the afternoon and evening while the House is sitting they are able to relieve the House of a large volume of business. The time spent by standing committees on an average of normal sessions is equivalent to sixty-five full working days in the House.

The Scottish Grand Committee. A further step in the process

of devolution was taken in 1948. In addition to the Scottish
Standing Committee there is now a Scottish Grand Committee, consisting of all the members representing Scottish
constituencies together with not less than ten nor more
than fifteen other members. Unlike the Standing Committee
the Grand Committee does not consider Scottish bills at
their committee stage but at their second reading stage;
it is also empowered to consider such Scottish Estimates
as may be referred to it and matters relating to Scotland.
But in whichever kind of business it is engaged, bill, estimate
or matter, the Scottish Grand Committee can take no
decisions. It can only report that it has considered the
business remitted to it by the House. The Grand Committee is thus in no sense a regional parliament in embryo.
Nevertheless, it performs a valuable function by enabling
Scottish affairs to be debated at length without encroaching
on the time of the House.

The Welsh Grand Committee. A Welsh Grand Committee
consisting of all the members sitting for Welsh constituencies together with not more than twenty-five others has
been set up in each session since 1959–60. This committee
is empowered to consider matters relating exclusively to
Wales on not more than four days, but not bills or Estimates.

<h3 style="text-align:center">THE GOVERNMENT TAKES THE TIME
OF THE HOUSE</h3>

After the great reforms of 1882 and 1888 there was not
unnaturally a certain respite. Nevertheless, from time to
time various minor improvements were felt to be necessary,
and in nearly every session some proposal was brought forward. It would be tedious to record them all in detail, but
one, though it was never adopted, deserves to be mentioned.
This was the suggestion that it should be possible to suspend

public bills from one session to the next. It was often found (and it still frequently happens) that a number of important bills are still under discussion when the end of the session arrives. Under the practice of the House such unratified bills die, with the result that much valuable time and work which has been spent on them is lost, and that if it is desired to persist in a measure it must be re-introduced afresh in the next session. In spite, however, of the recommendation of a select committee, specially appointed in 1890 to consider the question, the House has refused to change the rule in favour of public[1] bills. One of the main objections is that to permit a government bill to be proceeded with in the next session would deprive the Opposition of one of its strongest weapons.

Guillotine of Supply. In the eighties of last century there was a tendency for the discussion of the Estimates to occupy more and more of the time of the session – 9 sittings in 1860, 24 in 1884, and 27 in 1887. In 1888 the Hartington Committee suggested that as an experiment a part of the Estimates should be referred to a standing committee which was to discuss them in the same way as the Committee of Supply discussed them in the House. This proposal was not, however, adopted,[2] and it was not until 1896 that the solution was found which is substantially the procedure now used. In that year Mr Balfour proposed that the discussion of Supply should be limited to twenty days in the session. Any Estimates not discussed by the end of the nineteenth day were to be put to the vote notwithstanding. The proposal was accepted on an experimental basis as a sessional order. In 1902 it became a Standing Order. To compensate for this

1. It has been the practice of both Houses since the middle of the last century to suspend *private* bills.
2. But *see* p. 143.

restriction the Opposition have the right to choose the subject of debate. Another stage in the process of regulating the business of the House in the interests of the government had been taken. It was in effect an extension of the 'guillotine' to the business of supply. In 1947 twenty-six days were allotted to the business of supply, including Supplementary Estimates and motions 'That Mr Speaker do now leave the chair' on going into Committee of Supply.

Mr Balfour's Scheme, 1902 – Private Members' Time. In the succeeding sessions various measures were introduced piecemeal fashion. The discussion of each occupied much parliamentary time and in 1902 Mr Balfour resolved to bring in a comprehensive scheme which, it was hoped, would obviate the necessity for further reform for a considerable time. This scheme incorporated the new supply rule which, hitherto passed each session as a sessional order, now became a standing order. It also included a number of miscellaneous proposals for saving time, such as the presentation of bills without an order of the House. But by far the most important part of the scheme was that which regulated the sittings of the House. In order to obviate the necessity of carrying a motion on every occasion when the government needed more time, the permanent allocation of time for government business was greatly increased. The allocation of time for government business had risen from one Order day a week at the beginning of the nineteenth century to two days in 1837, and to three in 1852. Government business was now to have precedence at every sitting except the latter half of Tuesdays and Wednesdays and the whole of Fridays; the discussion of 'urgency motions' (*see* p. 138 above) was held over to the second half of the sitting; and matters of privilege, which hitherto could be raised at any time with seriously disruptive effects on the progress of business, were relegated to the Committee of Privileges.

The object of these proposals was very clearly to ensure that the government programme should suffer as little disturbance as possible, and the effect seemed so drastic as to merit the derisory name of 'the parliamentary railway time-table'. Mr Balfour's scheme has become the normal framework of business. In times of emergency, as during the 1914–18 war and from 1939 to 1949, the whole of private members' time was appropriated by the government.

In 1950, following the recommendation of the Procedure Committee of 1946, a new arrangement for private ('unofficial') members' business was introduced. Twenty Fridays after the Queen's Speech are set aside, 10 for motions, 10 for bills, precedence on these days being determined by ballot. The effect of this scheme was to give private members about the same number of days as they had before the war but less actual time.

Since the session 1959–60 an additional four half-days have been allotted to private members' motions.

CHAPTER X

THE COMMONS CONTROL
EXPENDITURE

I⊤ was the achievement of the Commons in the seventeenth century finally to establish their control over taxation. In the eighteenth they proceeded to establish control over expenditure. This objective they pursued along two lines. On the one hand the Commons sought to increase their control over *ordinary* expenditure by giving the king a regular income for the expenses of government, called the Civil List, and eventually establishing the right to control the use of it. On the other hand, by insisting on appropriating all *extraordinary* grants, the Commons brought into being the system of annual votes. These two lines of development converged – more and more of the ordinary civil expenditure was taken from the Civil List and either made a statutory charge on the Consolidated Fund or provided by annual vote. The final result was the twofold division of expenditure which we know to-day:

(*a*) charges upon the Consolidated Fund which are fixed by statute until parliament otherwise determines.

(*b*) expenditure which requires to be voted annually – the Navy, Army, Air and Civil Estimates, and the Estimate for the Ministry of Defence.

The Civil List, pruned at last of all purely governmental charges, eventually became merely the sovereign's income for his personal use – one of the items chargeable upon the Consolidated Fund. The establishment of the system of annual votes, though it does not cover the whole field of expenditure, is the basis of control over the executive by the House of Commons.

HISTORY OF THE ATTEMPT

The Civil List. Up to the time of the Restoration no systematic provision was made for the ordinary expenses of government. In times of peace the king was expected to live 'of his own', that is, from the revenues of the Crown lands and from tonnage and poundage which, originally granted for the Navy, had in time become a regular part of the royal income. The disposal of this income was, both in theory and in practice, entirely at the king's discretion. Since, moreover, the annual revenue accruing from these sources was fluctuating and uncertain, and so long as it might be supplemented from unparliamentary sources, it was impossible for parliament to attempt any systematic provision, still less to control its disposal. When, however, at the Restoration parliament established control over the sources of revenue, it became possible for, if not actually incumbent upon, parliament to make some more regular arrangement.

The Convention Parliament of 1660 estimated that £1,200,000 a year would be necessary and sufficient 'for the constant yearly support of his Majesty', i.e. for the ordinary expenses of government. Parliament did not, however, make a grant of this sum but proceeded to assign to the king such taxes as in their opinion would be sufficient to yield it. On this basis certain Customs and Excise duties were granted to Charles for life. When later in his reign it became apparent that these sources of revenue together with the lands and hereditaments of the Crown would not yield the estimated sum, the hearth and other taxes were added. Similar arrangements were made for James II, sufficient to produce the £1,900,000 which it was by then estimated was necessary.

The arrangements made at the Revolution were not fundamentally in advance of those made for Charles and

James, and in practice were rather less satisfactory. In 1689 the Commons asked for a statement of expenditure and receipts from the Auditor of the Receipt of the Exchequer and the Auditor of the Excise, and in the light of these statements resolved that the king should have an annual revenue in time of peace of £1,200,000, a sum which they knew was quite inadequate. But no bill was passed, and all that was done was to grant the king certain duties for three years for the expenses of the war. Similar casual arrangements were made from time to time during the rest of the reign. Certain of the Excise Duties were indeed granted for life, but the Customs which in the past had normally been regarded as part of the king's ordinary revenue were appropriated to the service of loans arising out of the war. It is not surprising, therefore, that William died in debt. In fine, at this period parliament had no clear idea what it wanted to do, and the only principle discernible in its financial arrangements was that the king should be kept short of money.

Queen Anne was treated somewhat better. At her accession she received certain duties for life which had been granted to William, minus a sum of £192,400 a year for what now came to be known as the Civil List, that is, the ordinary expenses of government. But, as in previous reigns, these arrangements were found inadequate, and additional provision for the Civil List had to be made. In 1713 the queen, being in debt, was authorized to borrow £500,000 on the security of certain duties.

It was not until the reign of George I that a fixed sum was provided for the ordinary purposes of government. At his accession he was given for life the same duties as had been given to Anne. As usual, the provision was inadequate, and in 1715 it was decided that some arrangement less casual than the methods hitherto employed to make up the Civil List expenditure was needed. It was estimated that an annual sum of £700,000 would be sufficient for this purpose, and certain sources of revenue were ear-marked to provide it. But, whereas on former occasions the Commons made no provisions to ensure that the sum required would be actually forthcoming, they now promised to make up any deficiency that might arise. Moreover, if a surplus should accrue, it was not to be applied to the Civil List, but to other purposes assigned by parliament. In fine, the Commons now controlled the total cost of government, though as yet no attempt was made to direct the expenditure of the sum allocated. Indeed, a proposal to call for a statement of Civil List expenditure was rejected by the Commons as derogatory to the Crown. It was another sixty years before such a proposal was accepted.

In 1769 George III was in debt to the amount of more than £500,000, and when he applied to parliament for assistance, proposals were made for the examination of the Civil List expenditure. Once more parliament refused to make so great a break with tradition. The debt was paid and the proposals were rejected on the ground that the Civil List was the king's own property, to be spent as he pleased. But in 1777, when the king was again in debt, parliament was in a less complaisant mood. The debt was indeed paid off and an additional £100,000 a year was granted, but only after accounts had been presented of the Civil List expenditure. The important principle that the Commons had a right to control the expenditure of the Civil List was thus conceded, and in the following years various attempts were made to establish it. In 1779 a motion to reduce the Civil List was rejected by the Lords. In 1780 the Commons claimed 'to examine into, and correct abuses in the expenditure of the Civil List revenues, as well as in every other branch of the public revenue'. In 1780 Burke brought in his scheme of 'economic reform', which, besides abolishing several offices and re-organizing others, included a detailed scheme for regulating Civil List expenditure. Later in the same year the Commons passed Dunning's famous resolution 'that the influence of the Crown has increased, is increasing and ought to be diminished', but they were unwilling to go to the lengths proposed by Burke; and in the following year they rejected a similar scheme. It was not until 1782 that the reformers gained their way. Lord Rockingham made it a condition of his taking over the ministry that the king should approve certain reforms, including that of the Civil List. Accordingly a scheme was brought in by the government and agreed to by both Houses. Certain offices were abolished, rules were laid down for the granting of pensions and for certain other branches of expenditure, and the Treasury was given control over the expenditure of the king's household. Most important of all, the Treasury was required to lay before the Commons within a year a list of all civil pensions and salaries, arranged in eight classes. Thus parliament definitely established its claim to control the ordinary civil expenditure.

The Consolidated Fund. So long as it was the practice to assign the produce of particular taxes for particular purposes it was impossible to take a comprehensive view of civil expenditure, and as a consequence a proper supervision of ordinary civil finance, whether by the Treasury or by parliament, was impossible. In 1715, when it was found necessary to provide an additional £120,000 for the Civil List, instead of granting such new taxes as might be thought sufficient to produce this sum, the Commons instituted a fund called the Aggregate Fund, to the support of which they assigned certain taxes and upon which they charged certain expenditure, including the £120,000 then needed to supplement the Civil List. In 1760 the hereditary revenues of the Crown were transferred to the fund and the whole Civil List was charged upon it. But a large amount of income and expenditure still remained outside the system, and it was left to Pitt in 1786 to create a single Consolidated Fund 'comprehending all the different branches of the revenue and liable to all charges which are now payable out of the same'.[1] Thus the whole of statutory expenditure as distinct from annual grants, including the National Debt and the Civil List, came to be charged upon a single fund. Grants of supply, however, still remained outside the system and continued for some time to be provided for directly out of the produce of specially allocated sources of revenue. Thus, for example, in 1813 out of £71,976,640 required to meet grants of supply only £500,000 was drawn from the Consolidated Fund. 'The rest of the ways and means required to meet the grants was provided by appropriating to them duties on malt, property, spirits, tea, tobacco, and various other war taxes, moneys raised by loan, by sale of Exchequer bills, by debentures, lotteries, and receipts derived from the sale of old stores.'[2] But by the middle of the century it had become the practice to place all the public revenue from whatever source to the account of the Consolidated Fund and to provide for all public payments, whether statutory or annually voted, out of that fund.

Appropriation. The idea of appropriating grants for specific purposes was at least as old as the fourteenth century. Thus, for example, in 1344 the Commons petitioned that the grant should be used for the purpose for which it had been asked. Attempts had also been made from time to time to enforce appropriation by the examination of accounts. But the real history of appropriation does not begin until after the Restoration. We have seen how the first attempt to make proper provision for the ordinary

1. 27 Geo. III, c. 13.
2. Report of the Select Committee on Public Moneys, 1857 (No. 279 of Session 2), Appendix, p. 25.

expenses of government was made in the reign of Charles II. In the same reign the Commons also began to improve their control over extraordinary expenditure by insisting upon appropriation.

In 1664 the Commons resolved that a sum of £2,500,000 'shall be raised in Three Years; and applied towards the maintenance of the Dutch war'; but the bill authorizing the raising of the supply contained no clause directing how it should be spent. In the following year the Commons inserted in a supply bill a proviso 'to make all the money that was to be raised by this bill to be applied only to those ends to which it was given, which was the carrying on of the war, and to no other purpose whatsoever, by what authority soever'. The innovation did not pass without comment. In the words of Lord Clarendon this clause was considered 'so monstrous, that the Solicitor and many others who were most watchful for the King's service declared against it as introductive to a commonwealth, and not fit for monarchy'. Nevertheless it was allowed to stand and the precedent was followed in subsequent years. A resolution of 1675 defined the purpose more precisely and prescribed a more stringent procedure: 'That the supply for building the ships shall be made payable into the Exchequer, and shall be kept separate, distinct, and apart from all other monies, and shall be appropriated for the building and furnishing of ships, and that the account for the said supply shall be transmitted to the Commons of England in Parliament.'

Examination of Accounts. Attempts to ensure regularity of expenditure by the examination of accounts are as old as the idea of appropriation itself. Thus in 1406 the Commons refused a grant until the accounts of the last grant had been examined. But such efforts were spasmodic, and it was not until after the Restoration that the Commons began to take a more continuous interest in the subject.

There was, indeed, an audit by officers of the Exchequer conducted under regulations framed in Tudor and Stuart times, and this went on unchanged for nearly a century after the Restoration. It was not a very satisfactory audit; in 1782 some twenty or thirty great accounts were still open, and there were accounts still unsettled of the reign of William III. Moreover, the audited accounts were not submitted to parliament; they were declared before, and passed by, the Treasury, whose authority was un-questioned.

Wars and the economic consequences of war have often provoked inquiries into expenditure. It was the second Dutch war which in 1666 prompted the Commons to demand the examination of the naval and ordnance accounts by a committee of their House with power to administer an oath. This was resisted by the Lords as an infringement of the prerogative, and parliament was prorogued before it could become law. In the succeeding session, however, the king, of his own motion, declared his willingness for the accounts to be examined, and a bill was passed for the appointment of a commission, which did not include any members of the House of Commons. The commission was empowered to take evidence on oath, to commit offenders against its orders, and to initiate proceedings in the Exchequer Court for the recovery of money misappropriated. But the lack of system in the national finances prevented the commission coming to any clear conclusion, and the only result of their labours was that the Commons blamed, and the Lords approved, the Treasurer of the Navy. The experiment was not tried again in the Stuart period. Nevertheless, though the result was unsatisfactory, the mere fact that it had been tried was a triumph for the Commons and is to be remarked as an early, if premature, attempt to bring expenditure to account.

Commissions of Accounts 1689–1715. The attempt was renewed after the Revolution. In 1691 a commission of nine members of parliament was set up to take the accounts of all the revenue since November 5, 1688, with power to examine any person on oath. This commission made a report of income and expenditure, but did not make use of the services of the Exchequer officers as they had been directed, with the result that they failed to make a genuine review of the national finances. Nevertheless, in spite of the manifest futility of this kind of inquiry, similar commissions were appointed each year till 1697, with no better success. They contented themselves with mere statements of income and expenditure without comment – information which could have been provided without their intervention. Such information as they obtained in virtue of their powers was used for party purposes.

During the reign of Queen Anne commissions of accounts continued to be appointed, but they had now become purely partisan bodies. Their labours served only to provoke quarrels between the two Houses, and their reports were used to make unfounded personal charges. Nevertheless, annual commissions continued to be appointed until 1714, when the Lords threw out a bill for this purpose. In 1715 the Commons themselves rejected a bill to appoint a commission. They had realized at last the futility, in the political circumstances of the day, of this mode of procedure, which was henceforth abandoned. It is to be noted, however, that the Commons successfully resisted every attempt by the Lords in this period to appoint as commissioners additional persons who were not members.

Non-parliamentary Committees of Inquiry. When next a demand arose for a financial inquiry, in 1780, Lord Shelburne, leading the Opposition in the Lords, proposed a joint committee of Lords and Commons. Such a proposal was open to the same objection of partisanship as the old commissions, and it was clear that the Opposition desired it less as a measure for securing economy or financial reform than as a means of restricting the influence of the Crown. The proposal was defeated, but the government, considering it advisable to make some concession to the evident desire of the House for financial reform, made the counter-proposal that a committee of seven persons, who were not to be members of parliament, should be appointed to examine the accounts of all persons entrusted with public money. The report of the committee, which was to be to the king and both Houses, was to include their observations on the fees and gratuities paid to those responsible for the collection and issue of public moneys, on the method of contracting for public services, and on the system of accounting. Power was given to the committee to examine on oath and to send for papers. This new non-parliamentary kind of committee was eminently successful. Similar committees were appointed in succeeding years, and in a series of reports between 1780 and 1786 recommended a number of improvements which were eventually adopted. They inaugurated in fact the financial reforms of the nineteenth century.

Select Committees on Financial Matters. During Pitt's administration a number of select committees of the House of Commons were set up to deal with various financial matters. But their terms of reference were limited strictly to specific tasks of immediate importance. Thus in 1786 a committee of nine members was appointed to examine the accounts of income and expenditure presented to parliament during that session, and to report upon the estimated future income and expenditure; and a similar committee was appointed in 1790 with the additional duty of reporting on the increase in the national debt. Other committees were appointed to inquire into the national debt in 1797 and 1798. Nevertheless, limited though these committees were in their objective and instituted as they were on the proposal of the government, they should be regarded as contributing, along with the non-parliamentary committee, to the movement towards financial reforms in the next century.

THE MODERN SYSTEM

Appropriation Accounts and the Committee of Public Accounts. The first of these reforms was brought about by the Act of 1802, which introduced 'Finance Accounts'. Up to this time there was no regular machinery for presenting to the House an over-all statement of expenditure. Returns of individual accounts might be called for and, as we have seen, committees or commissions of inquiry might be set up. But this was the first time in the history of English finance that an annual account of receipts into and payments out of the Exchequer was made.

These accounts, however, from the point of view of the House of Commons had one great defect. They did not show actual expenditure under each head but only the issues from the Exchequer under imprests to the several departments. Actual expenditure is made by the departments out of the imprests. This defect remained unnoticed till 1831, when Sir John Graham, in his speech moving the Navy Estimates, pointed out that 'The only remedy which he saw then was to lay before the House annually a balance sheet, in which would be specifically placed under each head the actual expenditure of the Navy and Victualling Boards.' In consequence of this speech parliament passed an act requiring the Admiralty annually to present such an account to the House of Commons. In 1846 a similar act was passed for the War and Ordnance Offices, but the Appropriation Accounts resulting from these Acts did not attract much attention from the House of Commons, and it was not until 1856 that, on the motion of Sir Francis Baring, a select committee was appointed to inquire into the receipt, issue and audit of public moneys in the Exchequer, the Pay Office and the Audit Department. The committee, strongly approving the method of Appropriation Accounts as applied to the Navy and the Army, recommended that it should be extended to the Civil and Revenue Departments, and that the whole of the resulting accounts should be presented to parliament before the end of the year after that to which they related. The committee further recommended 'that those audited accounts be annually submitted to the revision of a Committee of the House of Commons to be nominated by Mr Speaker'. The Committee reported in 1857, but it was not until four years later, in 1861, that Mr Gladstone, as chancellor of the exchequer, was able to carry the appointment of a permanent Public Accounts Committee. The remaining recommendations of the Committee were not implemented until 1866, when the Exchequer and Audit Act was passed. A year or more was spent on the organization of the Audit Office and in preparing the rules under which the several departments were to present their accounts to the Audit Office, and in 1869 the first complete audited accounts of the whole public service were laid before parliament.

The system instituted by the Act of 1866 has remained unaltered to the present day. By that act the old Comptroller of the Exchequer and the Board of Audit were replaced by a single officer, the Comptroller and Auditor General, who, though appointed by the Treasury, holds his office, during good behaviour, like a judge. His salary is charged not upon an annual vote, but upon the Consolidated Fund, and his responsibility is not to the government but to the House of Commons. His officers carry

out a continuous examination of the expenditure of departments and his comments arising from this examination are
embodied in reports which are made annually to the House
of Commons, and considered along with the Appropriation
Accounts themselves by the Committee of Public Accounts.
The Committee, in the light of these reports and their own
investigations, in turn report their observations to the
House. The reports are considered by the Treasury, in
order that effect may be given to the recommendations
which they contain, and these decisions are embodied in a
Minute which is communicated to the Committee. An
opportunity for discussing the Committee's reports on
Supply days is provided by standing order, and in 1960
the government undertook to set aside three Supply days
in each session for the discussion of the reports of the
Public Accounts Committee and the Estimates Committee
(*see* p. 166).

Annual Grants of Supply. The Revolution introduced
annual parliaments, and thereafter the practice of annual
grants came into regular use for war purposes. In the first
year of the reign of William and Mary, a bill was passed 'for
a grant to their Majesties of an aid of two shillings in the
pound for one year' in which a particular sum was appropriated for naval services, and very severe penalties were
inflicted upon the officers of the Exchequer if they should
permit any part of that sum to be applied in any other
manner than was specified in the Act. In the same way
specific sums were granted each year for the Navy, the
Army and the Ordnance services, and the same penalties
for misappropriation were re-enacted. During the War of
the Spanish Succession, indeed, undifferentiated lump sums
were sometimes granted, but the former practice was

restored after the Peace of Utrecht (1713). Thereafter the principle was firmly established and, although the exigencies of war sometimes necessitated deviations from the strict application of moneys to the purposes for which they were granted, the necessity for subsequent parliamentary approval sufficiently indicates that there was no doubt of the Commons' right to appropriate grants.

How real was the method of control is shown by the fact that after the Peace of Ryswick (1697) the Commons were able to insist upon a reduction of the Army against the wishes of the king. In the words of Hatsell, appropriation was made 'part of that system of government which was then established for the better securing of the rights, liberties and privileges of the people of this country'.[1]

The system of annual grants originated, as we have seen, in the demands for money for war purposes in the early part of the reign of William III, while civil expenditure was normally provided out of the Civil List. But even in this period a certain amount of civil expenditure was voted annually. At first the sums so granted were small, but, as new demands for the business of the central government and for the administration of the colonies arose, more and more items of civil expenditure came to be provided in this way. By the end of the reign of George III these sums had become substantial, and in 1843 the Miscellaneous Supply Services, which by that time had grown to several times as large an amount as the Civil List, were divided into seven classes which remained the basis of civil supply expenditure throughout the nineteenth century.

Estimates. From the moment that the system of annual grants in Committee of Supply was established, it was clearly desirable, if not actually necessary, to lay before the Commons estimates of the amounts needed. In the first

1. *Precedents*, Vol. III, 3rd Ed., p. 179; 4th Ed., p. 202.

year of his reign William III had estimates from the Army and Navy presented to them, and in the second session, at the request of the Commons, estimates for the ensuing year were presented by the Paymaster for the Army and by a Lord of the Admiralty for the Navy. The practice was followed in later years, though the Commons did not always ask for estimates. The Commons had not yet come to realize the value of estimates as an instrument of financial control. The subject is still somewhat obscure, but the number of soldiers and sailors required was decided in Committee of Supply, and the sum necessary to maintain them was sometimes discussed in some detail. The function of estimates at this period was less to provide a basis for criticism than an argument in favour of the grant.

It was a long time, however, before a detailed or complete system of Estimates came to be established. The first Army Estimate to be subdivided was that of 1711, when £3,162,687 was presented under seven heads. The Navy Estimates, on the other hand, were presented as a simple total until 1798. Detailed Navy Estimates were submitted in 1810, but no complete Estimates for the Navy were laid before parliament until 1819.

The systematization of the Estimates followed closely the correlative process in the Accounts. In 1832 the Navy Estimates and in 1846 the Army Estimates were presented in a form comparable with the Accounts, but it was not until 1866 that the Exchequer and Audit Act assimilated the whole system of Estimates to that of the Accounts.

Votes on Account for the Civil Estimates. These are necessitated by the fact that all grants are for the financial year only and all balances have to be surrendered at the end of the financial year to the Treasury. The departments require, therefore, statutory authority to carry on their services during the period of the financial year before their Estimates are voted. The practice of taking a vote on account for the Civil Estimates as a whole began in 1857. The Service departments do not need a vote on account because, unlike the Civil departments, they have power temporarily to apply money granted under one vote to a purpose covered by another. They are thus able to provide for the early part of the financial year by obtaining some of their votes in March.

Votes of Credit. In times of war, when large sums of money are needed for purposes which cannot be precisely defined, it has been the practice since early in the eighteenth century for the Crown to ask for votes of credit. They were frequently asked for in that century, usually for a defined amount, but on two occasions, in 1727 and 1734, without limit. In modern procedure the amount is always prescribed and is available only during the financial year in which the grant is made. They were used in the 1914–18 and the 1939–45 wars to provide only for services connected with the war, normal services being provided by ordinary Estimates.

Select Committees on Expenditure. By the establishment of the Committee of Public Accounts in 1861, and the system of account and audit in 1866, the parliamentary machinery for securing that money is spent on the objects for which it is voted was perfected. We have now to record the development of machinery for securing not merely that money is spent for the purposes expressed in voting the Estimates, but also economically and effectively.

The voting of supplies and the criticism of the demands made by the executive is the function of the House itself in the Committee of Supply. In the eighteenth century this function was exercised, at any rate on occasion. But the unsuitability of a body of more than 600 members for the scrutiny of the details of national expenditure must have been apparent from the beginning. In the early part of the nineteenth century, Joseph Hume, sitting in the House

every day and all day with his pocketful of pears, conducted
a tireless campaign for economy. But apart from Hume and
his little band of followers few members attended the Committee of Supply and fewer still took any interest in financial
matters. With the steady growth of public expenditure,
both in volume and complexity, and the increasing pressure
of legislation on parliamentary time, the Committee of
Supply tended during the nineteenth century to become
more and more an instrument for the criticism of administration rather than of finance as such. As a consequence of
this development a demand arose for some more apt
machinery for detailed scrutiny of the Estimates, and in
1888 a select committee was appointed to inquire into the
'procedure by which the House annually grants the Supplies
to Her Majesty'. The Committee of Supply was examined
from both points of view: as an instrument for securing
economy and efficiency in the public service by the examination of the Estimates, and as an opportunity for criticizing
the administration of home, colonial and foreign affairs.
The committee was, however, satisfied that the Committee
of Supply's exercise of both these functions was effective and
valuable, and contented itself with deprecating the reduction of the time spent in these ways. It made no recommendation calculated to improve the examination of the Estimates.
The problem remained unsolved, perhaps not fully realized.

The problem was taken up again in 1902, when a select
committee was appointed 'to inquire whether any plan can
be advantageously adopted for enabling the House, by Select
Committee or otherwise, more effectively to make an examination, not involving criticisms of policy, into the details of
National Expenditure'. This committee had no doubts about
the inadequacy of the Committee of Supply for this purpose
and declared themselves 'impressed with the advantages, for
the purposes of detailed financial scrutiny, which are enjoyed by Select Committees, whose proceedings are usually

devoid of party feeling, who may obtain accurate knowledge collected for them by trained officials, which may, if so desired, be checked or extended by the examination of witnesses or the production of documents'. No action, however, was taken upon this report, and it was not until nearly ten years later that the first Estimates Committee was appointed 'to examine such of the Estimates presented to this House as may seem fit to the Committee and to report what, if any, economies consistent with the policy implied in those Estimates should be effected therein'. A similar committee was appointed in 1913 and 1914 (without the restriction upon criticism of policy), but the experiment was not successful, and it was discontinued upon the outbreak of war.

In time of war no detailed Estimates of war services can be made. When therefore in 1917 the need was again felt for a body to inquire into the details of expenditure, a Select Committee on National Expenditure was appointed 'to examine current expenditure' whether contained in Estimates or in Votes of Credit (*see* p. 162 above). This committee was also empowered to make recommendations on the form of public accounts, the system of control within the departments, and the procedure of the House in relation to Supply and Appropriation, so as to secure more effective control by parliament over public expenditure. National Expenditure Committees were appointed in sessions 1917–20, in the course of which they examined the expenditure of a large number of different departments and carried out their duty to report upon the financial procedure of the House. They considered that the form of the Public Accounts and the Estimates was inadequate for any real control over expenditure, departmental or parliamentary. They pointed out that the Appropriation Accounts 'are accounts of the actual receipts and payments of the year in respect of the subjects to which the sums voted by parliament are appropriated, and differ from commercial accounts in this important respect: that all sums which have matured for payment in the year are, so far as physically practicable, actually paid'. Similarly the Estimate 'is one of the probable cash requirements only, or in other words, of the amount which it is anticipated will come in course of payment during the year and for which therefore provision must be made in the Budget'. In the phrase which was coined at a later date the nation's accounts are kept on the 'penny notebook' system, and this fact, coupled with the way in which expenditure is classed under Votes and Subheads and distributed between the departments, makes it impossible to determine from the Accounts or Estimates what the real total expenditure has been or will be on any particular object or project. The committee accordingly proposed a scheme for reorganizing the Estimates and Accounts so as to enable parliament and the departments themselves to know what the operations for which they are responsible actually cost. This scheme was applied experimentally to the Army Estimates, but it was not considered successful and was abandoned.

In 1919 the experiment was tried of sending Estimates to large Standing Committees of the type used for public bills. The procedure in these Standing Committees, unlike the procedure in a Select Committee, was to follow the customary procedure of the Committee of Supply. This experiment, designed as it was merely to save the time of the House, was unsuccessful. It was not continued,[1] and in 1921 a Select Committee on Estimates was appointed on the 1912 pattern with the addition of powers to report on the form of the Estimates. Estimates Committees were appointed every year until the outbreak of war, but largely for the same reasons that hampered the earlier Estimates Committees they did not provide an adequate solution of the problem of examining expenditure.

1. For reference of Estimates to the Scottish Grand Committee, see p. 143.

During the war of 1939–45, a Select Committee on National Expenditure again replaced the Estimates Committee. The National Expenditure Committees were empowered to appoint sub-committees and made full use of this power to cover as wide a field of expenditure as possible. The sub-committees had power to adjourn from place to place and were thus enabled to carry their investigations into the factories and shipyards. Since the end of the war, when the publication of complete Departmental Estimates was resumed, an Estimates Committee has been appointed each session. These Committees, profiting by the experience gained by the National Expenditure Committees in the use of sub-committees, have become a more effective instrument for the examination of expenditure than the earlier Estimates Committees. In 1946 one of the sub-committees conducted an inquiry in the British zone of Germany and was thus the first select committee to sit outside the United Kingdom; and in 1948 the House authorized another sub-committee to take evidence in Nigeria upon expenditure from the Colonial Development and Welfare Fund. Each report of the Committee receives a reply, which is published, from the Department or Departments concerned, and the reports may be discussed in the House on a Supply day (p. 159).

AUTHORITIES FOR CHAPTERS IX AND X

EINZIG, PAUL. *The Control of the Purse*, 1959.

HICKS, J. R. *The Problem of Budgetry Reform*, 1948.

HILLS, J.W., and FELLOWES, E. A. *The Finance of Government*. 2nd Edition, 1932.

REDLICH, J. *The Procedure of the House of Commons*. Vol. 1, 1908.

SELECT COMMITTEE ON NATIONAL EXPENDITURE, 1943–4. *Eleventh Report*.

SELECT COMMITTEE ON PROCEDURE, 1945–6. *Third Report*.

SELECT COMMITTEE ON PROCEDURE, 1959. *Report*.

CHAPTER XI

PARLIAMENT DELEGATES POWER
TO MAKE LAW

We can never be really in danger till the forms of Parliament are
made use of to destroy the substance of our civil and political liberties:
till Parliament itself betrays its trust by contributing to establish new
principles of government; and employing the very weapons committed
to it by the collective body to stab the Constitution.

THE LETTERS OF JUNIUS

Early Precedents. The practice of delegating the details of
legislation to the executive is as old as the fourteenth
century. A law of 1385 provided 'That the Staple should
be held in England; but in what places, and when it shall
begin, and concerning the manner and form of its regulation and government shall be presently ordained by the
king's council, with the authority of parliament; and whatever shall have been ordained in this part by the said
council, shall have the virtue and strength of parliament.'
The law bears a strong resemblance to a modern act of
parliament which gives to a statutory body the power to
make rules for the regulation of an industry.

A group of statutes of the reign of Henry VIII are usually
regarded as the historical ancestors of the modern type of
delegating statute. One of these, the Statute of Sewers of
1531, gave to the Commissioners of Sewers not only powers
to rate landowners, and to distrain and to impose penalties
for non-payment of rates, but also legislative power. It provided further that all statutes, acts and ordinances heretofore made by Commissioners of Sewers 'not being contrary
to this present Act nor heretofore repealed' are to 'be good

and effectual for ever', and that Commissioners hereafter to be named 'have full power and authority to make, constitute and ordain laws, ordinances and decrees, and further to do all and everything mentioned in the said Commission ... and the same laws and ordinances so made, to reform repeal and amend, and make new from time to time as the cases necessary shall require in that behalf'.

The most famous of the delegatory statutes of Henry VIII is the Statute of Proclamations of 1539. This enacted that the king with the advice of a majority of his council could issue proclamations which should have the force of an act of parliament. This has seemed to many a clear and striking case of parliament giving away its legislative power. But the power to issue proclamations for certain purposes had always inhered in the royal prerogative and they had in fact the force of law. Custom limited their use to occasions and purposes of an administrative character, and the statute of 1539 specifically provided that the common law, statute law, and rights of property could not be affected by proclamations issued under the Act. Seen in this light the Act appears not so much as the giving away of legislative power by parliament to the king, as defining more distinctly what the prerogative power should be able to do. Nor were the proclamations issued after 1539 notably different from those issued before. They dealt with coinage, prices, food, drink, cloth; vagabonds and aliens; war and peace – matters which it had always been considered possible to deal with by proclamation. What then was the necessity for the Act? The preamble gives two reasons. First, certain recent proclamations, particularly on religious matters, had been condemned. Secondly, sudden occasions may arise when some 'speedy remedy' is needed and there is no time to 'abide for a parliament'. The first is the historical reason, the need to define more closely the force of proclamations, the second is the practical reason which continues to justify the delegation of law-making power in modern legislation. Even so, contemporary opinion felt that the Act had gone a bit too far – it made it treason to disobey the Act and to leave the country to escape the consequences – and it was repealed in the first year of Edward VI.

The Statute of Wales (1542–43) contained a section which gave the king power to make laws for Wales, which 'shall be of as good strength and virtue and effect as if they had been had and made by authority of parliament'. This undoubtedly went further than any of the previous acts since in form it gave to the king the full law-making power which would ordinarily be exercised by parliament itself. But there were special reasons for this. The statute is in effect a comprehensive scheme for the administration of Wales. The object of the section in question was doubtless to enable the king to make such further provision for the reorganization of the country as experience might show to be necessary. It was repealed in 1642 because it was no longer needed. Once again, therefore, we must not regard the statute as giving away a power which parliament had habitually exercised in the past. It may perhaps be regarded as akin to that species of modern delegation which gives a Minister power to make regulations in order to bring an act into operation.

The Stuarts were less tactful than the Tudors in their attitude towards parliament, and we find less striking delegations of legislative power in the seventeenth century. They preferred to use the naked power of the prerogative to legislate, and this was one of the main complaints of the Petition for the Redress of Grievances in 1610:

It is apparent both that proclamations have been of late years much more frequent than heretofore, and that they are extended not only to the liberties but also to the goods, inheritances and livelihood of men ...

by reason whereof there is a general fear conceived and spread amongst your Majesty's people that proclamations will by degrees grow up and increase to the strength and nature of laws.

The fear that proclamations might be used to override parliament accounts for the fact that after the seventeenth century this useful means of delegating the details of legislation came to be neglected. As a consequence eighteenth-century acts of parliament tended to be overloaded with administrative detail.

One of the rare instances of the delegation of legislative power in the eighteenth century is provided by the Mutiny Act of 1717. The first Mutiny Act of 1689 had provided for the discipline of the army overseas, but the 1717 Act was the first to give the Crown express authority 'to make and constitute, under the Sign Manual, Articles for the better government of His Majesty's forces as well within the Kingdoms of Great Britain and Ireland as beyond the seas, and inflicting pains and penalties to be proceeded upon to sentence or judgment in Courts Martial'.[1]

More instructive from the point of view of the historical development of delegated legislation is an act of 1710. In consequence of an outbreak of plague on the Baltic, Queen Anne had issued a proclamation ordering a quarantine of all ships and persons coming thence, but, in order to enforce the proclamation, it was necessary to pass an act of parliament providing penalties, since at this date it had come to be held that a proclamation could not of itself create a new offence. Accordingly the Act gave the queen power to make regulations about quarantine, in order that she might be able to deal with similar situations in the future 'in a more expeditious manner than at present can be in the ordinary methods of the law'.

1. The power to make Articles of War has long been obsolete and the provision conferring this power was omitted from the Army Act, 1954.

The Modern Development. The Act of 1710 may be regarded as the true parent of the delegatory acts of the nineteenth and twentieth centuries. One of the earliest of these was an act of 1832 which originated in a similar necessity, that of dealing with an outbreak of disease more quickly than parliament could. 'Whereas', the preamble runs, 'it has pleased Almighty God to visit the United Kingdom with the disease called the cholera or spasmodic or Indian cholera, and whereas, with a view to prevent as far as may be possible by the Divine Blessing the spreading of the said disease, it may be necessary that rules and regulations may from time to time be established within cities, town or districts affected with or which may be threatened by the said disease, but it may be impossible to establish such rules and regulations by the authority of parliament with sufficient promptitude to meet the exigency of any such case as it may occur', the Privy Council is empowered to make rules and regulations for preventing the spread of the disease, relieving the sufferers and burying the dead. The Orders were to be published in the Gazette, which was to be evidence that they had been made, and were to be laid before parliament.

This act was the pattern for subsequent similar measures, such as the Act of 1847 for dealing with contagious or epidemic diseases, the Contagious Diseases of Animals Act of 1848, the Vaccination Act of 1858, and the Act of 1877 against the Colorado beetle. The practice which had been found so useful for dealing with outbreaks of disease was found useful also in other subjects where the same reasons of urgency did not apply. The Recovery of Small Debts (Scotland) Act of 1825 gave justices a power to make rules and orders 'for carrying into effect the provisions and purpose of this Act'. The Reform Act of 1832 gave power to appoint certain days and times in substitution for those specified in the Act, provided that the substituted days and times should 'be deemed to be of the same force and effect as if they had in every instance been mentioned in this Act'.

As the century progressed the practice of delegating legislative power tended to become more frequent, but the rate of increase was not regular. In 1860, 33 out of 154 statutes delegated powers (not necessarily all strictly legislative), but in 1880 only seven did so. In 1890 Statutory Rules and Orders first began to be printed in annual volumes by the Stationery Office, and since 1893 they have been methodically edited. From 1890 to 1900 the average annual output of Statutory Rules and Orders, General and Local, was just over a thousand. During the 1914–18 war the annual average rose to nearly 1,500, and in the three years after the war to 2,275. Thereafter the numbers settled down at about 1,500 a year until 1939, when the outbreak of war stimulated the output once again. The peak was reached with nearly 3,000 in 1942, after which the number tended to decline, and the present annual average is about 2,000. In time of peace the local Orders balance or outnumber the general, but during and after a war the general far outnumber the local.

The process of delegation was carried a stage further during the last war. Section 1 (1) of the Emergency Powers (Defence) Act, 1939, provided that His Majesty might, by Order in Council, make such Regulations ('Defence Regulations') 'as appear to him necessary or expedient for securing the public safety, the defence of the realm, the maintenance of public order and the efficient prosecution of any war'. Subsection (3) of the same section empowered the authorities and persons specified in the Defence Regulations to make orders, rules and by-laws for any of the purposes for which such Regulations are authorized by this Act'. The result was a kind of three-tier legislative process:

(1) the Act conferring the power to make Defence Regulations;

(2) the Defence Regulations conferring the power to make Rules and Orders;

(3) the Rules and Orders.

In a few cases the process was carried still further down to a fourth and fifth tier.

Parliamentary Control over Delegated Legislation. The extent of parliamentary control over statutory instruments (as Statutory Rules and Orders have been called since the Act of 1946 came into force) depends upon the enabling statute. From this point of view statutory instruments fall broadly into the following three classes:

(1) those which are not subject to parliamentary control at all;

(2) those which may be annulled if either House, within a period of forty days from the date of laying, resolves that an Address be presented to Her Majesty praying that the instrument be annulled;

(3) those which do not come into operation, or do not continue in operation beyond a prescribed period, unless approved by resolution of both Houses (in some cases of the House of Commons alone). These are called 'affirmative resolutions'.

It will be seen that the third category provides the most complete form of control, since instruments of this kind have to be put down on the order papers of (usually) both Houses and cannot become effective unless both Houses take some definite action upon them. Instruments in the first category are those which parliament has decided are of insufficient importance to require its oversight. The second category provides a kind of negative control – if the instrument is *not* successfully prayed against, it remains in force. The machinery of control has been the subject of some attention in recent years.

At the end of 1929 the Lord Chancellor appointed a

committee under the chairmanship of the Earl of Donoughmore to consider the whole question of powers exercised
by Ministers of the Crown, whether by way of delegated
legislation or judicial or quasi-judicial decision, and to
report 'what safeguards are desirable or necessary to secure
the constitutional principles of the sovereignty of parliament and the supremacy of the Law'. In their report this
committee stated that 'a system of delegated legislation is
indispensable' and gave six grounds upon which its use is
justified. It relieves the pressure on parliamentary time by
removing details of administration from acts of parliament.
It enables parliament to settle broad principles without
entering into highly technical details. It enables the
executive to provide for all the unforeseen contingencies
arising out of great schemes of reform without having to
return to parliament for amending acts or additional
powers. It enables the executive to deal expeditiously with
changes of circumstance, such, for example, as occur as the
result of scientific advance. It permits experiment and
amendment in the light of experience. It may be used to
arm the state with powers to deal with emergencies, of
which the Emergency Powers (Defence) Act of 1939 is
the classic example.

The committee also pointed to certain dangers. There
was the danger that, if the process of delegation were carried
far enough, it would amount to the executive assuming the
law-making function which properly belongs only to
parliament. The facilities afforded to parliament to scru-
tinize and control the exercise of powers delegated to
Ministers were considered inadequate. Delegated powers
might be so wide as to deprive the citizen of protection by
the courts against action by the executive which is harsh
or unreasonable. The committee made various recommendations to meet these dangers. As regards parliamentary
scrutiny, the committee recommended the setting up of a

committee by both Houses to consider not only every rule and regulation made under an act but also every act which gave law-making powers.

The proposal that acts which give law-making powers should be subject to scrutiny by a special committee has never been implemented. As regards instruments, the Lords had already in 1924 set up a 'Special Orders Procedure', but this deals only with those instruments which require affirmative resolution. Under this procedure a sessional committee examines and reports whether the provisions of an instrument raise important questions of policy or principle, how far they are founded on precedent, and whether there should be any further inquiry before the resolution is moved.

It was not, however, until the session of 1943–4 that the House of Commons began to set up a sessional committee for scrutinizing instruments. This committee, which followed closely the pattern suggested by the Donoughmore Report, is ordered to consider every statutory instrument upon which proceedings may be taken in either House, and to draw the attention of the House to any which impose charges, are not open to challenge in the courts, make unusual or unexpected use of the powers conferred, have retrospective effect, have been unjustifiably delayed in publication, or require elucidation. The object of this committee is not to inquire into the merits of instruments, but rather to ensure that the attention of parliament is called to certain objectionable features of delegated legislation which have long been the subject of public criticism.

The Select Committee on Statutory Instruments also from time to time makes special reports dealing with particular aspects of the making, laying and publishing of instruments. As the result of one of these special reports, and in fulfilment of one of the recommendations of the Donoughmore Committee, the procedure as to the printing, publishing and laying of instruments was laid down afresh by the Statutory

Instruments Act, 1946, which replaces and amends the Rules Publication Act of 1893. The most important change made by this Act is that it standardizes the period during which instruments are subject to annulment. Hitherto the period had varied from 21 to 100 days and there was no uniform method of computing the number of days. The period now laid down for all instruments subject to annulment, whether made under an existing or a future Act, is forty days, not including any time during which parliament is dissolved or prorogued or during which both Houses are adjourned for more than four days.

It will be observed that the procedure of the House of Commons only provides opportunities for considering statutory instruments at the moment when they are made. No procedure exists for considering instruments after they have come into force and experience has been gained of their working. In 1953 a select committee considered, among other suggestions, a proposal that petitions for redress of grievances arising out of instruments should be considered by a body of three members, to be called Triers of Petitions, who were to have power to hear witnesses and to report whether action should be taken to remedy a grievance. It was also proposed that special facilities should be given for the House to debate such reports. The select committee, however, rejected these suggestions on the ground that members already had opportunities for raising grievances and it was unnecessary to provide any special procedure for dealing with those arising from statutory instruments.

AUTHORITIES FOR CHAPTER XI

ALLEN, C. K. *Law and Orders*, 1945.

CARR, C. T. *Delegated Legislation*, 1921.

COMMITTEE ON MINISTERS' POWERS. *Report*, 1932. Cmd. 4060.

SELECT COMMITTEE ON DELEGATED LEGISLATION, 1952–53. *Report*.

CHAPTER XII

THE SECOND CHAMBER

> There be but two erroneous opinions in the House of Commons:
> That the Lords sit only for themselves, when the truth is, they sit as
> well for the Commonwealth. The second error is, that the House of
> Commons are to begin to give subsidies, yet if the Lords dissent, they
> can give no money.   SELDEN

IF the Commons have occupied the main part of our attention, that is inevitable, since the history of parliament is in
fact one of the gain in power and function of the Commons
and the corresponding decline in the sphere of activity of
the Lords. Beginning as the single, undifferentiated organ of
government in all its aspects, the king's Great Council has
shed some functions and been restricted in others. As the
advisers of the king and the body from which his ministers
were drawn, the place of the Lords was taken first by the
Privy Council and later by the Cabinet. In the matter of
finance the initiative passed early to the Commons and control was finally surrendered entirely to them. The legislative and judicial functions of the Lords have come to be
restricted partly as a result of constitutional change, partly
by deliberate enactment. Of this progressive loss of function
some indication has been given in the chapters dealing
with the growth of ministerial responsibility and the winning
of financial control by the Commons. In this chapter it is
proposed to outline the process whereby the Great Council
became the House of Lords, then to complete the account
of its financial and legislative powers, and finally to outline
the history of its judicial functions.

THE COMPOSITION OF THE HOUSE OF LORDS

IT had always been the right of kings to summon to their
great councils whom they would, and the notion that a

special writ of summons to the Model Parliament of 1295 entitled its recipient and his successors to be summoned to every future parliament is without historical foundation. Something like a hereditary peerage had indeed emerged by the end of Edward I's reign, but it carried no right of parliamentary summons. A peer was one who had the right to be judged by his fellow vassals in the king's court and the right to judge his vassals in his own. There were peers whom the king did not summon, some he summoned occasionally, and there were others, like the judges, whom the king regularly summoned, who were not peers. The possession of lands in chief from the king gave him a special claim in feudal right to call such tenants for advice, and tenancy in chief may have been the ground upon which the practice of summoning the spiritual lords was also based. But in any case, tenancy in chief conferred only a special liability, certainly not a right. Richard II first created dignities by letters patent and these were hereditary, but there was nothing in them (as there is now) about a hereditary right to sit in parliament.

There was never any doubt that all the bishops should be summoned. For the Model Parliament and regularly thereafter writs were sent to the two archbishops and the nineteen bishops – fifteen of English sees, four of Welsh. The list continued unchanged until Henry VIII created six new bishoprics.

Edward I sent writs to seventy abbots and priors in 1295 but Edward II never summoned so many as sixty. In the course of the fourteenth century an increasing number obtained exemption from attendance. After Edward III the number summoned fell to twenty-seven (less than one in ten of the whole number of abbots in the country), and remained constant at this figure throughout the fifteenth century. It is not without significance that, except for two priors and two Augustinians, all those who continued to be summoned were Benedictines from royal or reputedly royal foundations. In 1513 the judges declared that the presence of the abbots was not essential to parliament, but seventeen are shown as present in the picture of 1523 (*see* Plate 1). In 1539, when the larger monasteries were surrendered to the king, the abbots disappeared from parliament.

The summons to the lay lords was more variable than that to the spiritual. Eight earls and forty-one barons were summoned to the Model Parliament, but in the last eight years of Edward I's reign the basis of summons seems to have been the armed host summoned to Carlisle in 1299. This list consisted of 11 earls and 104 other magnates, many of whom were not barons. In the reign of Edward III the lords in parliament consisted of about 50 earls, barons and bannerets, most of whom had made their name in France. In the fifteenth century the number steadily rose to a maximum of 73 in the parliament of 1453-54 – the last before the outbreak of civil war. The effect of the wars was to reduce the number of lords, whether by death or attainder or royal selection, so that in the first parliament of Henry VII there were only 36 [1] lay lords. The right to a place in the Lords had by this time become hereditary. Henry VII summoned 4 new men, Henry VIII added about 20 more, and by the end of Elizabeth's reign the number who might be summoned had reached 60.

Apart from the reversal of the proportion of lay to spiritual peers, resulting from the dissolution of the monasteries, the Tudors made little essential change in the composition of the House. Henry VIII might suggest to a particular peer that his obedience to a writ of summons was unnecessary, but there was no question of manipulating the

1. Including four who appear not to have received a writ of summons.

composition of the House whether by royal creations or by withholding writs of summons. The first Stuart king was in this as in other matters less scrupulous to maintain the outward form of constitutionality. James I instituted the practice of selling dignities. Baronies were sold for £10,000 each, viscounties for £15,000 and earldoms for £20,000. The motive of these transactions, however, was financial rather than political. At these prices the market was good – James added fifty-four lay peers to the House – and it is clear that a peerage had come to be regarded as a desirable prize.

During the Civil War the Commons had resolved that the House of Lords was 'useless and dangerous', but in 1657 Cromwell proposed a new House of Lords without bishops. The Commons insisted that in the writs this assembly should be called 'the other House of Parliament'. When Cromwell in his opening speech addressed the parliament as 'My Lords and Gentlemen of the House of Commons' the Commons raised a great storm, and soon afterwards the parliament was dissolved. In the following year Richard Cromwell summoned a parliament which also included the 'Other House'. This lasted only a few weeks and no more was heard of the 'Other House'. The sixty summoned consisted of some who had been peers before the Rebellion, members of ancient families (of whom some were ennobled after the Restoration), and men who had rendered outstanding service to the Commonwealth or the Protector.

The Restoration. The abolition of feudal tenures soon after the restoration of the House of Lords in 1660 marked the changed view of peerage more distinctly. In medieval times tenancy in chief of the king had entailed the duty of counsel, 'suit of court', and, with the abolition of feudal tenure as a qualification for peerage, the duties attached inevitably disappeared also. Suit of court was indeed preserved in general terms, but what the act conferred specifically was a 'right to sit' in the House of Lords. There was no mention of any duty to attend in parliament. Henceforward peerages became the reward of political service to a party and the House of Lords began to acquire the character which predominates to-day.

The wholesale creations of James were not imitated by his successors. Charles II created 60 peerages, but at his death the House numbered no more than 181 members. At the time of the Revolution the House of Lords consisted of about 150 lay and 24 spiritual lords. By the accession of George I the number of lay lords, including now the 16 Scottish representative peers, had risen to 194, making a total membership of 220. For the greater part of the eighteenth century the number remained fairly constant at about this figure, new peerages balancing extinctions.

The Peerage Bill, 1719. Reference has already been made to the occasion in 1712 when a predominantly Tory Ministry, having negotiated the Peace of Utrecht with the support of a majority in the Commons, found itself threatened in consequence by the opposition of a Whig majority in the Lords. To remove the deadlock Anne created twelve Tory peers, thereby turning a minority into a majority. This use of the prerogative naturally aroused the criticism of peers of longer standing, and in 1719 a bill was introduced to secure 'that the number of Peers of Great Britain on the part of England' should never be enlarged by more than six. The bill had not reached third reading when parliament was dissolved, but a similar bill in the following session was decisively defeated in the Commons by the eloquence of Robert Walpole. 'How', he asked, 'can the Lords expect the Commons to give their concurrence to a bill by which they and their posterity are to be for ever excluded from the peerage?' Had the bill passed, the

Crown would have been deprived of the constitutional means by which a deadlock between the Houses could be resolved. In the crises over the Reform Bill and the Parliament Bill the threat of creating peers was used with similar effect.

From the accession of George III a very great increase was made in the size of the House. In his first Ministry Pitt created nearly ninety new peerages; by 1830 the number of peers had risen to about 400. The precedent set by Pitt was followed, and the number of new creations steadily exceeded extinctions. By the end of the century the House numbered 591. At the present time more than 900 persons are entitled to a writ to attend.

Representative Peers. The Act of Union with Scotland (1707) added sixteen representative peers who are elected by all the peers of Scotland. They sit during the life of the parliament for which they have been summoned. Non-representative peers may not sit in the House of Commons. Since the established Church of Scotland is Presbyterian, no provision was made for spiritual lords.

The provisions of the Act of Union with Ireland relating to the House of Lords differed in several respects. Twenty-eight representative peers were to be elected for life, and the remainder were eligible to sit in the House of Commons. Unlike Scotland, where no new peerages were to be created, provision was made for keeping the peerage of Ireland up to the number of 100. An Irish peer who is elected to the House of Commons is not entitled to the privileges of peerage, nor may he be elected as a representative peer or vote at any election of representative peers. Since the constitution of the Irish Free State in 1922 there has been no election of representative peers to fill vacancies, and the last of them has died. Four Irish spiritual peers were provided for by the Act of Union, but these lost their seats in the House of Lords when the Church of Ireland was disestablished in 1869.

Life Peerages. Though, as we have seen, the hereditary basis of the summons to the lay lords only became established in the course of centuries, the possibility of breaking away from the hereditary principle seems not to have been seriously considered until 1856. In that year, by way of strengthening the House of Lords in its judicial capacity, Queen Victoria directed the issue of letters patent purporting to create Sir James Park (who had been one of the barons of the exchequer) Baron Wensleydale and a peer 'for and during the term of his natural life'. The Lords Committee of Privileges, however, resolved 'that neither the said Letters Patent, nor the said Letters Patent with the usual writ of summons, enable the grantee to sit and vote in parliament'. This resolution was endorsed by the House, and to resolve the difficulty, new letters patent were issued creating a hereditary barony in the usual form.

Soon after the Wensleydale case it was proposed to create two judges life peers, and in 1870 a wider proposal was made to confer life peerages on men distinguished in any form of public service, but neither suggestion was accepted. It was not until 1877 that the principle of the life peerage was successfully carried into effect on a limited scale. Power was given to appoint two Lords of Appeal in Ordinary, with further power to add a third on the death or resignation of two paid judges of the Judicial Committee of the Privy Council and a fourth on the death or resignation of the two remaining paid judges. The Lords of Appeal in Ordinary were to hold office subject to good behaviour, but could be removed on the address of both Houses of Parliament. They were to rank as barons during their lives, but they were to be entitled to sit and vote only so long as they held office. This limitation of the right to sit and vote to the period of tenure of office revived a principle which had not been applied to laymen since the days of the early Chancellors, but it was removed eleven years later. The Lords of Appeal in Ordinary [1] thus became lords of parliament for life without their titles descending to their heirs. In 1958 the principle was extended by restoring to the Crown the right to confer a life peerage on any person, man or woman; there are now (1963) 36 life peers and 7 life peeresses, excluding the Lords of Appeal in Ordinary.

THE FINANCIAL AND LEGISLATIVE
POWERS OF THE HOUSE OF LORDS

As we have seen (in Chapter V), the claim of the Lords to amend money bills was effectively abandoned in the seventeenth century; and since 1860 their power to reject proposals for taxation has been destroyed by the Commons' practice of embodying all the financial provisions for the year in a single bill.

The right of the Lords to reject a bill other than a money bill had never been questioned, and until 1831 this right had been exercised by the Lords without producing irreconcilable conflict between the Houses. In that year the Lords rejected the second Reform Bill. The recent elections had been fought and won by the Whigs on the issue, 'The Bill, the whole Bill and nothing but the Bill'. The government therefore felt justified in using extreme methods to enforce their policy and threatened to create sufficient peers to carry the bill. A third bill was introduced in 1832, and the Lords gave way. This event could not but considerably affect the legislative power of the Lords for the future. The position was clearly stated by Lord Lyndhurst in a debate on the admission of Jews to parliament in 1858: 'It is also a most important part of our duty to check the incon-

1. Nine were authorized in 1947. *See* p. 194.

siderate, rash, hasty and undigested legislation of the other House', but not to make 'a firm, determined and persevering stand against the opinion of the other House of Parliament when that opinion is backed by the opinion of the people.' Similar opinions were expressed by the Marquess of Salisbury in 1869 on the second reading of the Irish Church Bill. Since Scotland, Ireland, Wales and, 'though more doubtfully and languidly', England were in favour of the bill, he considered that the House of Lords would not be doing its duty if it opposed itself further against the will of the nation.

The Parliament Acts, 1911 and 1949. Such views of the rights of the Lords in regard to legislation were typical of enlightened constitutional thought in the nineteenth century, and no serious conflict arose between the Houses. But in 1906, when a Liberal Government came into power, events made it clear that some stricter definition of the powers of the Lords was needed. Between 1906 and 1910 eighteen out of 213 government bills failed to pass into law. Not all the eighteen bills were rejected outright by the Lords, but several were so heavily amended by them that they were abandoned. Five of the bills which failed to pass were of first class importance in the view of the government: an education bill, a plural voting bill, a Scottish land-holding bill, a licensing bill and a finance bill. In 1907 the Commons resolved that the power of the other House to alter or reject bills passed by this House 'shall be so restricted by law that within the limits of a single parliament the final decision of the Commons shall prevail.' The conflict was brought to an issue when the Lords rejected the Finance Bill in November, 1909. It appeared that the Lords were willing to re-open even the question of the financial supremacy of the Commons, which seemed to have been settled in 1860. The Commons declared the action of the Lords to be a breach of the constitution and a usurpation of privilege. Parliament was thereupon dissolved, and the elections resulted in a majority determined to settle the issue with the Lords. An attempt to reach agreement by a compromise between the leaders of the great parties in both houses failed. In this *impasse* the Prime Minister, Mr Asquith, advised the king to dissolve parliament on the understanding that, if a substantial majority in the new parliament was in favour of the government policy, he would be 'ready to exercise ... the prerogative of creating peers, if needed, to secure that effect shall be given to the decision of the country'. The strength of parties in the new House of Commons was almost the same as in the previous parliament, and the government considered themselves justified in reintroducing the Parliament Bill. The Lords, after a little hesitation, bowed to the threat to swamp their House and passed the bill.

The financial provisions of the Parliament Act are designed to debar the Lords from rejecting or amending 'money bills'. A 'money bill' which has been passed by the House of Commons must become law within one month of its being sent up to the Lords, whether or not they have agreed to it. A 'money bill' is defined as one which the Speaker has certified as concerned only with taxation, charges on the Consolidated Fund or on moneys provided by parliament, or the raising of loans. These financial provisions hardly advanced the position of the Commons, since they merely enacted with precision what the Commons had already substantially secured since 1860 by embodying the budget of each year in a single composite bill. Their value consists in their providing a regular method for enforcing the financial supremacy of the Commons without conflict with, or coercion of, the Lords.

The provisions of the Parliament Act in regard to other bills mark a much greater constitutional change. All other public bills (with the sole exception of one to extend the life of a parliament), which have been passed by the House of Commons in three successive sessions (whether of the same parliament or not) and thrice rejected by the Lords, shall become law, upon the third rejection, provided that at least two years have elapsed since their original second reading in the Commons. The general idea that the Lords ought not to persist in thwarting the clear will of the nation had often been expressed by reasonable statesmen. But the circumstances in which the will of the Commons ought to prevail had never been precisely defined. That a non-financial bill should become law without the assent of one House was a constitutional innovation for which there was no historic basis as there was in the case of money bills.

The power of the Lords to delay a Commons bill was further curtailed by the Parliament Act of 1949. This Act reduced the number of sessions in which a bill objected to by the Lords must be introduced and passed by the Commons from three to two, and the period of time which must elapse between Second Reading in the Commons in the first session and Third Reading in the Commons in the second session from two years to one year.

The Parliament Bill of 1949 was itself passed into law under the provisions of the original Parliament Act. Only two other acts have so received the Royal Assent without the consent of the Lords: the Government of Ireland Act, 1914, and the Welsh Church Act, 1914.

The Bryce Conference, 1917. The preamble of the Parliament Act stated the intention at some future time 'to substitute for the House of Lords as it at present exists, a second chamber constituted on a popular instead of a hereditary basis'. Various attempts have been made to redeem this promise. The most important of these was the appointment in 1917 of a conference under the chairmanship of Viscount Bryce, to consider the legislative powers appropriate to a

Second Chamber, the composition of such a Second Chamber and the best mode of adjudicating differences between the Houses. The Conference found four functions appropriate to a Second Chamber: the revision of bills brought from the Commons; the initiation of bills 'of a comparatively non-controversial character'; the delaying of bills, especially those affecting the constitution, 'to enable the opinion of the nation to be adequately expressed'; and the 'full and free discussion of large and important questions' in an atmosphere removed from the exigencies of party government. For the performance of these functions, it was agreed that a Second Chamber ought not to have equal powers with the House of Commons. In particular it should not have the power of making or unmaking ministries or enjoy equal rights in dealing with finance. The prime quality required was a moral authority deriving at once from the eminence of its members and its superiority to factious motives. The most difficult question the Conference found was the composition of such a body. The method adopted was a compromise between two principles: capability and experience on the one hand, and responsibility to public opinion on the other. Three-fourths of its members were to be elected by the House of Commons on a geographical basis; the remainder were to be chosen by a joint standing committee of both Houses. At least thirty of those in the latter category were to be peers or bishops. Membership of both sections was to be for twelve years. For the adjustment of differences between the two Houses, a reversion was recommended to an improved kind of free conference, a procedure which had become obsolete.

The proposals of the Bryce conference were not implemented. From time to time proposals for reform have been discussed in the Lords' House, notably those sponsored by Mr Lloyd George's government in 1922 and Mr Baldwin's government in 1927, but none has been accepted. Since the restriction of the Lords' legislative powers, the question of reforming the constitution of their House has lost urgency. The business of the House is carried on by a small number of peers supplemented from time to time by those who are interested in a particular debate. From this point of view the revival of the right of the Crown to create life peers (*see* p. 184) may be regarded as a measure of reform. It may enable people who would refuse a hereditary peerage to play a useful part in the work of the Upper House. The payment since 1957 of an allowance for the expenses of attendance has the same end in view.

THE JURISDICTION OF THE HOUSE OF LORDS

Origin. The judicial function of the House of Lords is at once the oldest and the most characteristic. When William conquered England there was no supreme court of law. The local courts of shire and hundred were independent in their own sphere. William initiated that process of centralization in all matters of government, including justice, by which he laid the foundation of a national state in this country. It was the great work of Henry II to complete the centralization of justice. The effect of his reform was to transfer a large area of jurisdiction from the courts baron to the *curia regis*. Such an accession of business in an age when so much litigation was concerned with land could hardly have been undertaken by a court which combined with its judicial functions all the other functions of government as well. Accordingly, at the same time that he was building up the central jurisdiction of the *curia regis*, Henry II provided for the devolution of the actual work of justice by establishing, in 1178, a body of five judges who were to be a supreme tribunal in all legal questions. This court was the parent of the Court of Common Pleas.

While the Court of Common Pleas was attracting to itself much of the superior jurisdiction which would otherwise have fallen to the *curia regis* itself, other courts were growing up and gathering to themselves other parts of its jurisdiction. At first the King's Bench is hardly distinguishable from the *curia regis*. From the fifth year of the reign of Richard I to the end of the reign of Henry III the rolls of the *curia regis* record without distinction the business of the King's Bench and Common Pleas, but from the first year of Edward I separate rolls were kept. The Chancery Court originated in the writs issued by the Chancellor under the Great Seal and the Exchequer Court similarly grew out of the Treasurer's Department. In 1279–80, as we have seen, provision was made for sorting petitions, which were, of course, all addressed to the king, into five bundles, to be considered respectively by the Chancellor, the Exchequer, the justices, the justices of the Jewry, and the king in council. Only petitions of special difficulty were to be reserved for the king in council and resulted in *placita* in parliament. But the *curia regis* was not a court of appeal. Its most characteristic function was to 'move' the courts and to direct them to give judgment without delay – not always successfully. This control over the courts by means of directions before judgment continued at least as late as the reign of Edward III. A typical instance of this 'moving' the courts is recorded in 1339–40, when, in response to the petition of a suitor in the Court of Common Pleas, it was 'agreed by all in full parliament, and command was given by the Prelates, Earls, Barons, and others of the parliament to Sir Thomas de Drayton, Clerk of the Parliament, to go to the Justices of the Common Bench and to tell them either to proceed with the case or, if they could not agree, to bring the rolls and the record into parliament.' The latter was done. The process and record were read in parliament and judgment given 'upon advice having been had as well of the Prelates and Magnates, as of the Justices and others of the Lord and King being in full Parliament'.

From the reign of Henry IV onwards the original jurisdiction of the *curia regis* declined. On the one hand the petitions presented by the Commons from the early part of the fourteenth century onwards became the basis of legislation. The petitions of individuals to the king in council, on the other hand, which were more suitable for judicial decision, were diverted to the courts. This was a marked feature of the Tudor period, when much of the judicial functions of the *curia regis* was delegated to the prerogative courts of Star Chamber and Requests. In the first seventeen years of James I's reign only one writ of error was brought before parliament.

In the Stuart period the ancient process of impeachment in which the Commons presented the accusation and the Lords were judges was revived (*see* Chapter VI). The House of Lords, as the inheritors of the jurisdiction of the *curia regis*, took the opportunity presented by this revival to assert a claim to be the highest court in the land. In Charles II's reign they went further and claimed an appellate jurisdiction, a claim which was the more easy to justify since the abolition by the Long Parliament of the prerogative courts of Star Chamber and Requests. The Commons did not at once concede this claim and asked for evidence to support it. The Lords retorted by asking for evidence of the Commons' claim to the exclusive control of supply. In the end a compromise was reached, each house conceding the other's claim. The appellate jurisdiction of the House of Lords remains to-day and has been regularized by the Act of 1876. In civil matters there is an ultimate appeal to it from all courts in the United Kingdom of Great Britain and Northern Ireland. In criminal matters there is an appeal to it from the Court of Criminal Appeal upon a certificate from the Attorney General that a point of law of exceptional public importance is involved.

At the same time that they established their appellate jurisdiction, the Lords abandoned all claim to original jurisdiction. Since 1666 they have not claimed an original civil jurisdiction, but in criminal matters original jurisdiction survived until recently in respect of peers. For the right to be tried by his peers was the essential quality of peerage and was confirmed by the 39th Article of Magna Carta. Privilege of peerage in criminal proceedings was abolished by the Criminal Justice Act, 1948.

The Judges in Parliament. These changes in the jurisdiction of the House of Lords were not unnaturally reflected in the varying position of the judges in parliament. In the reign of Edward I they had been members of the *curia regis* as fully as any earl or baron summoned thereto. But, as the tendency of specialization proceeded and the Courts of Exchequer, King's Bench and Common Pleas came less and less to be committees of the Council and more and more to be independent courts of law, the legal specialists began to lose their place in the parent institution. About 1345 the judges of the three courts ceased to be sworn members of the Council. In the time of Richard II they were still assessors and advisers of the Council for legal purposes, and so continued late into the reign of Henry VI. In the fifteenth century most of the judges of the King's Bench and Common Pleas, certain king's serjeants-at-law and the king's attorney received writs of summons, but the only parliament for which we have an attendance list (that of 1461) seems to indicate that they were not normally present at the deliberations of the Lords. The two chief justices and the other judges were present on the woolsacks at least ceremonially in 1523 (*see* Plate 1). But the Act of 1539 'for placing of the Lords' makes no reference to the judges and laid down that no one under the degree of baron, even the Lord Chancellor, who had a place in the parliament chamber in virtue of his office, 'could have any interest to give any assent or dissent in the said House'; and in 1586 the Commons resolved that 'though the chancellor and the judges were competent judges in their proper courts yet they were not in Parliament'. From this time onwards the judges could come into parliament only when their advice was required. Thus in 1660 it was ordered by the House of Lords 'that the Lord Chancellor do move his Majesty that he would be pleased to give order for writs to the Judges, whereby they may attend in the House as Assistants'. This is their position in modern times. The Lords can always call for their assistance and have frequently done so, especially in cases of privilege.

The reduction of the judges to the position of assistants by no means rendered their influence in parliament negligible. From the earliest times they must have taken a leading part in the drafting of acts. In 1305 the chief justice told counsel: 'Do not gloss the statute. We understand it better than you, for we made it.' In Henry VII's reign the judges sitting together formulated the main principles of bills before they were introduced in the Commons or the Lords, and in the time of Henry VIII it was the custom of the Lords to obtain copies of bills introduced in the Commons and to seek the opinion of the judges upon them.

In Stuart times the subservience of the judges to royal influence after Coke's removal from the bench resulted in further reducing their status, and in that period the Lords were not anxious to have their advice. In the eighteenth century they continued to receive a writ of summons to each new parliament and were in fact consulted on points of law at least in the first three-quarters of the century. But when a proposal was made to consult them in 1778, the Earl of Shelburne remarked that there were few questions which their Lordships could not decide as well as the judges and refused to 'go to Westminster Hall [where the courts then sat] to inquire whether or not the constitution was in danger'.

Though the position of the judges in parliament was thus both formally and actually reduced to insignificance, it must not be supposed that the legal element was entirely eliminated from the House of Lords nor that its judicial business was in the hands of a purely lay body. There were in the eighteenth century always a large number of distinguished lawyers in the House of Lords. There were the Chancellor, any ex-Chancellors and such judges as had, like the great Lord Mansfield, received a peerage. Until 1873 indeed the appellate jurisdiction of the House was exercised by the whole body of peers, and every peer had the right to attend and give judgment. But from the beginning of the eighteenth century it began to be recognized as inappropriate that a peer without legal qualifications should take part in such business and in practice it was generally left to the lawyers. In 1873 the Lords of Appeal in Ordinary were instituted. These Lords of Appeal in Ordinary, of whom nine were authorized in 1947, are barons for life. Together with the Lord Chancellor and any peer who has held high judicial office (including that of judge of the Supreme Court) they conduct the judicial business of the Lords. The wheel has come full circle. The position of parliament as the highest court in the land is firmly established and its efficiency ensured by the inclusion of the greatest men of law in it.

AUTHORITIES FOR CHAPTER XII

PIKE, L. O. *Constitutional History of the House of Lords*, 1894.
TURBERVILLE, A. S. *The House of Lords in the XVIIIth Century*, 1927. *The House of Lords in the Age of Reform, 1784–1837, with an Epilogue on Aristocracy and the Advent of Democracy, 1837–1867*, 1958.

CHAPTER XIII

THE SECRET GARDEN OF
THE CROWN

In the twentieth century administration is still what it was in its
origin: the secret garden of the Crown.   PAUL DE VISSCHER

WE have tried to give the reader, not a history of parliament, but a historical account of certain of its leading
principles and features. It is an extraordinary history. It is
certainly not the tale of steady constitutional advance to
which our schoolmasters have accustomed us. Looking
back on the long-drawn-out processes by which each advantage was won, we cannot but be struck, not only by the
intense conservatism of Englishmen in constitutional
matters, but by the apparent indifference to the value of
the progress already achieved. It is understandable perhaps that contemporaries should not be able to see which
way the road must lead and excusable that they should
tread it with hesitation. But to refuse to exploit, and to
neglect and even to throw away the advantage already
gained, seems folly.

At the very moment when the Commons had secured for
themselves the most fruitful of the principles of Magna
Carta – the principle of consent to taxation – they mini-
mized its power for consitutional progress by exercising it
as rarely as possible. When they discovered the value of the
right to petition and seemed well on the way to a monopoly of legislation, they surrendered the initiative to the
Crown without a struggle. Their very privileges they owed
as much to the artful complaisance of a tyrant as to their
own exertions.

Even the aggressive political consciousness of the seventeenth century seems almost to have been ashamed of its exuberance and shrank from using the opportunities for reform which the ascendancy of parliament conferred. Such admirable proposals for electoral reform as those of 1647 and 1653 came to nothing, and the anomalies of the system (already recognized by James I as due for reform) continued, or rather increased, for the best part of two centuries. Cromwell's brave experiment of the 'Other House' was received without enthusiasm, and the constitution of the House of Lords still awaits reform.

Later centuries showed hardly more sense of the future. The principles of ministerial responsibility and party government, those twin pillars of the modern parliamentary system, were abhorred by most respectable statesmen of the eighteenth century. The tradition of the Speaker's neutrality, of which British parliamentarians are justly proud, is hardly a century old and owes more to the outstanding character of one or two holders of the office than to any general recognition of its necessity. It would seem indeed as if the Commons had made progress in spite of themselves.

Certainly our constitutional conservatism has its compensations. As Lord Acton has said, 'The one thing that saved England from the fate of other countries was not her insular position, nor the independent spirit, nor the magnanimity of her people ... but only the consistent, uninventive, stupid fidelity' to the political system. We have had a civil war without a proscription and a revolution without bloodshed. We have had our share of demagogues, but no one has succeeded in establishing a tyranny. For all this we may be justly thankful and take a share of the credit. Nevertheless, when we look back over the story, we cannot but recognize how much more we owe to our good fortune than to our own exertions.

Can our luck hold? Can we hope that in this age we shall

be surely and safely led to the solution of our constitutional problems by a series of providential accidents? Hardly, since, in an age of impersonal government and pervasive bureaucracy, personality counts for much less, and against these forces only a constant and devoted jealousy for parliamentary rights can avail. In fact, the price of liberty is more certainly than ever political vigilance, and, if the point needed illustrating, the recent history of other nations is ample evidence that the wages of political neglect is slavery.

The story we have told is the story of the process by which parliament has slowly, but never too surely, improved its control of the government. Parliament originated in the attempt of the magnates to make good their claim to be consulted on great matters of state, and early in the fourteenth century the claim was fully established. Meanwhile, the Commons had arrived and were beginning to take a share in legislation. The fifteenth century was a period of consolidation rather than of advance, for when our records begin in the next century the main outlines of procedure are already laid down. In the sixteenth century the liberties of the Commons were conceded, and in the seventeenth they gained sole control of taxation. In the eighteenth and nineteenth centuries the theory of ministerial responsibility was worked out, and the Commons became more truly responsive to the will of the electorate. In the nineteenth century also procedure was modernized and a technique developed for the control of expenditure. What is to be the special contribution of the twentieth century?

It is not difficult to see where the contemporary problem lies. Generically, it is the problem of adapting the methods of parliament to the changing business of government. At various times in the past the administration of justice, the regulation of trade and industry, ecclesiastical settlement, foreign policy and administrative reform have been the main concern of government. In the twentieth century social welfare and economic control have increasingly taken their place. The inauguration of such schemes requires legislation and, to the extent that their outline is prescribed in acts of parliament, the House of Commons retains its traditional method of control – its ordinary procedure for the consideration of a bill. But the operation of such schemes and their implementation in actual practice, these are matters of administration. And from the point of view of the citizen it is the details of administration that matter. Is the procedural machinery of the House of Commons adequate to control the details of administration?

By the reorganization of the Accounts government finance was put on a proper basis, and by the institution of the Comptroller and Auditor General and the Public Accounts Committee the House has secured that money is spent on the purposes for which it is intended. By this reform it may fairly be claimed that the House has completed its machinery for controlling expenditure from that point of view. But control of expenditure in any full sense of the expression means something more than merely ensuring financial regularity – fundamental though that must be. After assuring itself that the money granted has been spent on the purposes for which it was intended, parliament naturally demands that the money shall be spent on those purposes wisely, without waste and to the best advantage. By the system of annual Estimates which have to be voted in Committee of Supply, the House of Commons, in theory at any rate, has created the opportunity whereby the proposed expenditure of a department in any year can be investigated. In fact, as we know, the Committee of Supply has never been an efficient instrument for this purpose. A Committee of the whole House, it was originally designed to enable the whole body of members to discuss fully and informally the grants for which they were asked by the government and the conditions they might wish to attach to such grants; it was never intended to be an instrument for the close and continuous examination of expenditure; and Joseph Hume was perhaps the first and the last member to use it primarily for this purpose. Consequently, the House has been obliged from time to time to appoint special committees to inquire into this or that branch of expenditure, and since 1912 it has regularly [1] appointed a committee to examine the Estimates, and to suggest what economies may be possible, consistent with the policy implied therein.

Several points are worth noting about this development of the House's machinery for controlling expenditure. By delegating the examination of the detail of expenditure to a select committee the House has done much more than merely save parliamentary time by entrusting some of its work to a small number of members 'upstairs'; it has virtually invented a new way of exercising its responsibility. By giving the task to a select committee, the House recognizes, by implication at any rate, that the detail of expenditure is a task which should not involve party issues. The Estimates Committee are empowered to consider how the policy implied in the Estimates may be carried out more economically. Secondly, by giving to the Estimates Committee power to send for persons, papers and records, it is recognized that for the purposes of financial investigation the method of debate on the floor of the House is unsuitable and that the detailed information needed to carry out such a task properly can only be provided in memoranda and elucidated by the examination of expert witnesses. Thirdly, and this is perhaps the most important aspect of this technique, the House has virtually admitted that, though in principle the minister is responsible for every action of his

1. Except in time of war, when complete Estimates were not available. See Chapter X.

department, however small, and must be prepared to defend it, in actual practice the execution of the policies of the department is the work of his permanent officers and they, as the real authors of administrative decisions, are in the best position to explain them. In this way, the principle of ministerial responsibility is retained unimpaired, while the House has adapted its methods to the practical realities.

So far it may be said that the House of Commons has adapted its methods to the increasing volume and complexity of governmental expenditure and, to that extent, the House has improved its control of one aspect of administration. But the expenditure shown in the annual Estimates is a very imperfect basis for the control of administration in general. Not only are the financial responsibilities of the government much wider than the sums shown in the Estimates indicate, but there is much administrative activity which cannot be well related to expenditure and cannot be properly judged from a financial point of view.

By the custom of the House it is permissible to discuss the whole of a minister's responsibility to parliament on the Vote for his salary. In this way it is possible to raise any administrative question in Committee of Supply, even though it has little or no genuine financial implication. But, as we have seen, the Committee of Supply has serious limitations as an instrument of detailed inquiry. Moreover, the Estimates Committee, bound as it is by its order of reference to the Estimates, is precluded from investigation into administrative activity which is not at least indirectly reflected in expenditure. The House has, however, one instrument which may be regarded as specially adapted to the raising of administrative points unconnected with finance – the question hour. For an hour each day on four days a week members may put questions (of which they have given previous notice) to ministers on any matter falling within their several responsibilities. Through questions the House has a most useful means of raising quickly and publicly any administrative short-comings, and this right is one of the private members' most treasured parliamentary weapons. Nevertheless, the limitations of the method must be recognized. It is suited to single points such as can be raised within the ambit of a single Question and answered in a few sentences. It offers little opportunity of setting the matter in its true context and encourages the insidious rather than the penetrating question, the slick rather than the convincing reply. It is a spotlight which, if correctly aimed, may reveal administrative weakness, but it cannot thoroughly illumine a matter of any size or complexity.[1]

In these circumstances, it would appear that the House of Commons is hardly better provided with opportunities for criticism of non-financial aspects of administration than of financial. Can other means be provided? Apart from the practical question of finding time for exercising the function, the main difficulty seems to be the lack of a peg on which to hang such criticism. Administration consists in a vast number of departmental decisions of varying importance embodied in minutes and memoranda, letters and circulars. All of these decisions are ultimately covered by the authority of some statute, but none is embodied in a form which automatically brings it within the purview of the House of Commons. Each decision is merely a thread in a seamless web of administration. There is, however, one category of administrative acts which is of necessity embodied in a document and falls within the purview of parliament. These are those rules, orders and regulations, generically called statutory instruments, which provide the legal

1. For a novel method of dealing with the grievances of individuals against the executive see *Occasion for Ombudsman* by T. E. Utley, 1961.

framework of much administrative activity. It is usual to inaugurate schemes of social welfare or projects of public enterprise by means of an act of parliament which specifies the purposes proposed and prescribes the form of administrative machinery for carrying them out. The precise method of carrying out the purposes is not specified in detail – the administration of the scheme or project being left to the department or statutory body charged with this duty. The general authority to do what is necessary (within certain limits and safeguards) to achieve the required purpose does not, however, empower the department or statutory body to make rules and regulations. This power is specifically conferred by a separate section of the act which prescribes the form of parliamentary control applicable to them. The various degrees of control which may be laid down have been described in an earlier chapter. Whatever form of procedure is provided, the general effect is to give opportunities for preventing an objectionable regulation from coming into force. From that point of view the 'Prayer' procedure, whether of the affirmative or negative kind, and the examination by the Select Committee on Statutory Instruments are valuable checks. Neither, however, provides a satisfactory opportunity for judging the statutory instrument in its full context and in the light of experience of its operation, since both these checks are applied within a few days of its presentation to parliament. In other words, the existing procedure is hardly adapted for considering a statutory instrument as the thing it really is – an instrument for carrying out the purposes of a statute. The House, it would seem, preoccupied with the legislative aspect of statutory instruments, has provided itself with a procedure adapted to deal with them from this point of view, but has failed to recognize that they are from the practical point of view much more closely akin to administration – they are, in fact, the legal framework of administration. From this point of view, it would seem possible to develop a method of control similar to that which the House has developed for control of the detail of expenditure. Already, as in the case of expenditure, the House has armed itself with the machinery needed for ensuring what we may call the formal regularity and propriety of statutory instruments – that is the duty of the existing Select Committee. But the House has not yet found a satisfactory way of ensuring that statutory instruments efficiently carry out the purposes for which they are made – nothing corresponding to the kind of inquiry which the Estimates Committee makes into the question whether the sums authorized have been efficiently spent. The criteria of efficiency of course are different. In the case of expenditure, the question is simply: is the best value being obtained for the money? In the case of a statutory instrument, or more probably a corpus of statutory instruments all relating to a single scheme, the questions would be: do the statutory instruments achieve what they are intended to do, do they do it in the most equitable way and with the minimum inconvenience to the citizen compatible with achieving the purpose?

We come last to the most difficult of the problems confronting the House in its effort to control the administrative aspects of government. We refer to those public corporations which manage industries and utilities on behalf of the nation. Let it be said at the outset that here no question is raised of the ability of the House of Commons using its traditional methods to control the major policies of such corporations and to hold the appropriate minister responsible. The administration of such enterprises, however, is in quite a different case. The problem is complicated by two factors: first, such corporations, though responsible for administering large amounts of state property, may not receive any support from public funds and, as a consequence, no trace of their administrative activity may appear in the Estimates. Secondly, these corporations, being semi-independent bodies, are not, like the department for which a minister is responsible, his servants – but rather his agents acting on his behalf within the framework of only the broadest directives. Consequently, the minister cannot be held responsible for the day-to-day administrative acts of the servants of the corporation in the same direct way as he can be for the acts of officers in his department. There thus arises the anomalous situation that a minister is responsible to parliament for administering a part of the national estate and yet is not directly answerable for the details of administration.

In recent years there has been much discussion of the problem of parliamentary control of nationalized industries, and in 1957 a select committee was appointed 'to examine the Reports and Accounts of the Nationalized Industries'. This committee has produced a number of valuable reports, from which three points clearly emerge. First, it can no longer be doubted that there *is* a legitimate field of inquiry for a select committee, which encroaches neither on the government's responsibility for public policy nor on the directing board's for commercial policy. Secondly, the facts collected and elucidated by these inquiries have been of great value to the House when it debates the nationalized industries. Above all, the committee has shown that parliamentary control of nationalized industries can be conducted in a non-party atmosphere.

These are some of the problems of parliamentary government in the twentieth century. They are all variations of the same theme: how is parliament to discharge its responsibility for controlling the administrative aspects of government? The solution of these problems will be the subject of the next chapter in the history of the English parliament.

INDEX